ROBERT BLOOMFIELD

SELECTED POEMS

Robert Bloomfield

Pub. by Vernor & Hood Poultry, Jan 1. 1802.

ROBERT BLOOMFIELD

Selected Poems

Edited by John Goodridge and John Lucas

with an Introduction by John Lucas

TRENT EDITIONS

Published by Trent Editions 1998

Trent Editions
Department of English and Media Studies
The Nottingham Trent University
Clifton Lane
Nottingham NG11 8NS

The cover illustration is Sapiston Church, from E.W. Brayley, *Views in Suffolk, Norfolk and Northamptonshire* (1806), opp. p. 36. The frontispiece is that of *Rural Tales* (1802), first octavo edition. Other illustrations are taken from early editions of the poems they illustrate.

Printed in Great Britain by Goaters, Nottingham
ISBN 0 905 48894 6

Contents

Preface

Our first priority in this selection of Bloomfield, given his general neglect and the lack of modern editions of his poetry, has been to fit in as much poetry as we could, including the whole of *The Farmer's Boy*, and a generous selection of the later material, especially the narrative poetry, which we regard as greatly undervalued. The material is grouped in such a way as to indicate the general sequence of publications in Bloomfield's lifetime and incorporate posthumously published texts in the approximate order of composition.

There are textual problems with Bloomfield's poetry, particularly *The Farmer's Boy*. Bloomfield regarded Capel Lofft's prefatory material and editing as intrusive, and in the stereotype edition of his first four volumes, *The Poems of Robert Bloomfield* (two volumes, 1809), he took the opportunity to correct the text, and in some cases restore manuscript readings. We have chosen to follow this edition, rather than the more familiar first editions, as our copy text for *The Farmer's Boy*, *Rural Tales*, *Good Tidings*, and *Wild Flowers*. *The Banks of Wye* follows the text of the corrected second edition of 1813, and *May-Day with the Muses* follows the text of the first edition (1822). Other texts are from Bloomfield's *Remains* (1824). Since this is a general reading edition, we have silently corrected obvious typographic errors and inconsistencies in printed texts, especially where line-end punctuation is unclear, and have generally standardised the use of emphasis and quotation marks in line with modern practice. We have carefully examined the manuscripts and early editions, and recognise that a full presentation of variant texts is beyond the scope of this edition, and that a complete scholarly edition of Bloomfield is urgently needed.

Bloomfield was an attractive prose writer, and we have included many of the Prefaces he wrote for various editions of his work, which speak eloquently of his hopes, fears and progress as a poet. Like his later contemporary John Clare, Bloomfield is usually a very accessible poet, and we have therefore felt able to keep our editorial commentary to a minimum, preferring to be generous with his words than with ours.

We are grateful to Mary Dawson and Celia Coates (Nottingham Trent University, Library and Information Services), for their help, to the British Library (Department of Manuscripts), the Houghton Library, Harvard University, and Northamptonshire Central Library for allowing us to consult materials in their keeping, to Barry Bloomfield and Bob Heyes for their generous suggestions and assistance, and to Alison Ramsden for her proof-reading.

Chronology of Bloomfield's life

1766 (3 December) Robert Bloomfield born in Honington, Suffolk. His father George was a poor tailor, his mother Elizabeth a village schoolteacher. His father died of smallpox before his first birthday.

1777 Sent to the farm of his uncle, William Austin, in nearby Sapiston.

1781 (29 June) Joins his brothers George (a shoemaker) and Nathaniel (a tailor) in London, staying with George, running errands and learning his trade.

1784 Trade dispute among the shoemakers; Bloomfield returns to the country, staying with William Austin; returns to London.

1786 (24 May) 'A Village Girl' printed in *Say's Gazetteer*, sets up on his own.

1790 (12 December) Marries Mary Ann Church.

1796 (May) Begins composing *The Farmer's Boy*.

1800 (1 March) *The Farmer's Boy: A Rural Poem* published by Vernor and Hood, introduced by his patron, Capel Lofft.

1802 *Rural Tales, Ballads and Songs* published; (July) befriended by Edward Jenner.

1803 Given a clerical post by his patrons, but his health forces his resignation after just a few months. Sings a 'Song' for Jenner's birthday.

1804 *Good Tidings, or News from the Farm: a Poem* published; (December) Bloomfield's mother dies

1806 *Wild Flowers; or, Pastoral and Local Poetry* published.

1807 Tour of the Wye valley and the Welsh border country.

1808 *Nature's Music: Consisting of Extracts from Several Authors, with Practical Observations and Poetical Testimonies, in Honour of the Harp of Aeolus* published, assembled and edited by Bloomfield, one of whose entrepreneurial activities in this period was to make and sell aeolian harps.

1811 *The Banks of Wye: a Poem* published.

1812 Leaves London and moves to Shefford, Bedfordshire.

1815 *The History of Little Davy's New Hat* published, a prose work for children,

1822 *May Day with the Muses*, his final volume of poetry, published.

1823 *Hazelwood Hall, a Village Drama, in Three Acts* published.

   Bloomfield died on 19 August, in poverty and distress (but there is *no* evidence of mental illness, *pace* the *Dictionary of National Biography* and later sources). His friend Joseph Weston edited the *Remains of Robert Bloomfield* (two volumes, 1824) for the benefit of Bloomfield's family.

Introduction

Robert Bloomfield's fame died before he did.[1] There is of course nothing unusual in that. It's the fate of many poets. And the posthumous reputations of deserving poets may take years to develop. Auden famously remarked that some bad poets may be undeservedly remembered but that no good poet is undeservedly forgotten. This may be true in the long run but Bloomfield's wait for recognition has been longer than most. During the nineteenth century editions of his poems went on being reprinted. My own copy of his *Works*, dated 1867, is by no means either the first or last of the single volume 'Complete Editions' brought out by George Routledge and Sons. Bloomfield must have had his readers.

But just who these readers were is something of a mystery. They certainly don't seem to have included professional poets. I can find no evidence that his work made an impact on Browning, Tennyson, or any of the noteworthy poets of the latter part of the nineteenth century. William Barnes, who was twenty-three when Bloomfield died, must surely have known the work. Yet as far as I know Barnes does not register the fact. At the end of my copy of *The Works of Robert Bloomfield* comes a clutch of 'Poetical Tributes', the first of which is an 'Epistle', said to be 'From Roger Coulter, of Dorsetshire, to his friend Giles Bloomfield, the Suffolk Farmer's Boy.' It begins:

VRIEND GILES,
> When vust I heard thy tunevul voice,
> I stood ameaz'd, an' star'd, and gaped awoy: —
> That can't be Stephen, Ned, nor Hodge, I cried;
> When some oone zaid—'why, that's the Zuffolk Buoy.'

Roger Coulter, whoever he may be, could not have read Barnes, although his dialect is that of Wessex. And as no date is given for his 'Epistle', it could have been written during Bloomfield's lifetime (it was published posthumously, in 1824). Bernard Barton's 'On The Death of Robert Bloomfield', on the other hand, was clearly written after the poet's death. Barton, known as 'the Quaker Poet', ends his elegiac stanzas with the hope that 'long may guileless hearts preserve / The memory of thy verse and thee.' Barton may not have intended the note of condescension, but there is here a tacit admission that Bloomfield's poetry is unlikely to have lasting appeal for sophisticated readers. 'Peace to the bard whose artless store / Was spread for Nature's humblest child.' With friends like Barton Bloomfield hardly needed enemies.

This is not to say that Barton damaged Bloomfield's posthumous reputation by unintentionally writing him off as a *naif*. Later writers are unlikely to have gone to Barton to find out how they should regard Bloomfield. It's more the case that Barton was voicing what became a commonplace assumption. And from *naif* to neglected proved to be a short step. The only exception seems to have been W.H. Hudson who, according to Edward Thomas, liked 'a vast range of English poets from Swinburne to Bloomfield.'[2] But by the time Thomas was writing, in *A Literary Pilgrim in England*, 1917, editions of Bloomfield's *Works* had long dried up. As a result, and with due allowance made for a selection produced in 1971 by William Wickett and Nicholas Duval and published by a small press, Terence Dalton Ltd. of Lavenham, Suffolk, the present selection is the first of any importance to appear in the last fifty years.

It was *The Farmer's Boy* which made Bloomfield famous and even brought him money. And it was probably with that poem uppermost in mind that Barton claimed Bloomfield, 'though free from classic chains, / Our own more chaste Theocritus.' Bloomfield is here praised for being a 'natural' poet. He is free of what Edward Young had years earlier called the encumbrances of the 'scholar poet', those chains of learning and, therefore, 'the notions of others'. Bloomfield is instead a type of the natural genius: 'crossing all public roads into fresh untrodden ground.'[3] He is therefore assimilable to the tradition from which Burns misleadingly claimed to come and whose starting point was typically thought of as being Theocritus. Theocritus, the first pastoral poet, told the truth. Later poets, such as Virgil, who self-consciously acknowledged a debt to Theocritus, were by comparison, artificial. So at least ran a line of argument through the eighteenth century. Hence Richard Polwhele's remark, made as early as 1692, that 'The pieces of Theocritus are the result of his own accurate observation, he described what he saw and felt. His characters, as well as his scenes, are the immediate transcript of nature.' This claim, which Polwhele makes in the Dissertation and Notes to his two volume *Idyllia, Epigrams and Fragments of Theocritus, Bion and Moschus*, establishes a template for later assumptions about Theocritus.[4] And this is why John Clare called Bloomfield 'the English Theocritus.'

I have elsewhere suggested that when Clare uses this phrase he means to celebrate Bloomfield as the true recorder of English rural life in its pre-lapsarian state, that is, before enclosure came 'and made the poor a slave.'[5] Here, we need to understand that *The Farmer's Boy* is by no means as innocent of art as Barton and Clare imply. Bloomfield was a very self-conscious artist. In later life, when he was casting about for ways of easing his financial difficulties, he considered that 'some Country tales, and spiced with love and courtship, might yet please, for Rural life by the art of Cooking may be made a relishing and highly flavour'd dish, whatever it may be in reality.'[6] And you cannot read very far in *The Farmer's Boy* without recognising that it is an extremely successful blend of several kinds of rural poem. One such kind is what we might call neo-Theocritean poetry, the most distinguished example of which is Thomson's *The Seasons*, although Stephen Duck's *The Thresher's Labour* is crucial in the attention it pays to unglamorous, daily work. Hence, to take one example among many, Bloomfield's account in 'Spring' of the 'clatt'ring Dairy-Maid immers'd in steam, / Singing and scrubbing midst her milk and cream, / [who] Bawls out, "Go fetch the Cows!"' (ll. 165-7), where pastoral 'sweetness'—artifice—is dispelled by terms such as 'clatt'ring' and 'bawls'. Hence, too, Bloomfield's description, also in 'Spring', of the ridge-and-furrow method of ploughing:

But, unassisted through each toilsome day,
With smiling brow the plowman cleaves his way,
Draws his fresh parallels, and, wid'ning still,
Treads slow the heavy dale, or climbs the hill. (ll. 71-5)

John Barrell helpfully points out that this method of ploughing was accomplished by 'ploughing a land down its centre-length, and turning then in an ever-widening arc at the ends of the lands, and throwing the mould of ploughing soil always towards the centre of the land.'[7]

Yet we are entitled to feel that the source for the propriety of these lines on ridge-and-furrow ploughing is less Theocritus than Virgil. And certainly the kinds of practical husbandry addressed in the *Georgics* are replicated in *The Farmer's Boy*, as for example where Bloomfield speaks of Giles foddering cattle on 'The sweet nutritious turnip' ('Winter', l. 24), a root vegetable which with the increasingly widespread use of crop rotation, had become part of the staple winter provision for beasts. This is not to say that Bloomfield would have read Virgil or Theocritus—and certainly not in the original. His formal education was scanty and by his mid-teens, after some years working on a farm, he was in London, helping his brother at the trade of cobbling. It is, however, apparent that as a young man he must have studied Duck, Thomson, and their many imitators, as well as Goldsmith, whose *Deserted Village* is another felt presence in *The Farmer's Boy*.

To put matters this way is perhaps to give the impression that Bloomfield's poem is a kind of palimpsest. If so, I need to remark that *The Farmer's Boy* is remarkably successful in adapting a variety of styles and genres in order to make a poem which, if not *sui generis*, brings real distinction to the various traditions out of which it emerges. It is easy to point these traditions out. And, given that Bloomfield 'had worked hard to learn the proper language of poetry', we can as easily identify sources for particular words and phrases.[8] The 'grateful scene' of the farmyard in 'Spring' (l. 185) has its source in Book Four of *Paradise Lost* ('Cheer'd with the grateful smell old Ocean smiles'); the description of advancing Spring spreading 'Flow'rs of all hues, with sweetest fragrance stor'd; / Where'er she tread, Love gladdens every plain' (ll. 272-3) comes from Pope's 'Where'er you tread, the blushing Flow'rs shall rise, / And all things flourish where you turn your Eyes'; and behind the 'ruffian winds' that cannot 'shake' the waters in 'Autumn' (l. 26) are those 'rough winds' that shake the darling buds of May.

So one could go on. To do so, however, would not diminish Bloomfield's accomplishment. *The Farmer's Boy* most adeptly blends various stylistic registers. Moreover, Bloomfield's serviceable couplets, end-stopped though they mostly are, have sufficient flexibility to allow him to snap rhymes neatly shut or, more usually, develop small narratives. He apparently first thought of writing the poem in unrhymed verse after the manner of Thomson, whose Miltonic style abounds throughout, but changed his mind because he composed most of it in his head while working at his cobbling trade and found it easier to commit the poem to memory once he'd chosen to rhyme it.

This isn't surprising. Nor should we be surprised to find that *The Farmer's Boy* feels to be made up of small narrative blocks—it might be better to call them sequences—which between them illustrate seasonal life on the farm. Such life is often presented as 'simple', a word Bloomfield uses on more than one occasion. When he does so he seems to be assuring his readers that the rural scene is preferable to that of the Metropolis, which in 'Spring' he more or less anathematises as the place where 'Art':

Her poring thousands stows in breathless rooms,
Midst pois'nous smokes, and steams, and rattling looms;
Where Grandeur revels in unbounded stores;
Restraint, a slighted stranger at their doors! (ll. 239-42)

'Art' means manufacture but it also means Artifice as the enemy of simplicity. The lines are both subtle, witty, and deeply hostile to the city. The 'poring thousands' are those who bend to the machines, but we must also feel that they pore over delusive dreams of success. 'Breathless rooms', while literally meaning workplaces shut against light and air also, by transferred epithet, suggests rooms where gulled workers are 'breathless' with excitement at their vision of golden futures. It is for this, we might even think, that they have *poured* into the metropolis. But the gap between rich and poor is epigrammatically caught in the disdain shown by Grandeur for Restraint. That couplet sets up a kind of anti-pastoral. The unbounded 'stores'—the word inevitably suggests granary or rooms teeming with food—are closed to the 'slighted stranger', that hallowed supplicant or beggar, who according to the custom of the country, is never sent away empty handed ('Where comes no guest, but is allowed to eat, / Without his fear, and of the lord's own meat', as Jonson had put it in 'To Penshurst').

The claims of hospitality are on more than one occasion invoked in *The Farmer's Boy*. The opening lines of 'Winter' extol the virtues of that 'bond of amity and social love' (l. 8), where it is suggested that such love extends even to animals: 'To more than man this generous warmth extends, / And oft the team and shiv'ring herd befriends' (ll. 9-10). Here, 'generous warmth' is syntactically detached from human agency. It is simply 'there'. But in an all-important passage in 'Summer' Bloomfield places it in the context of the 'long-accustom'd feast of Harvest-Home' (l. 290). Here, the 'careful dame, / And gen'rous host invite their friends around'. In this extended passage (lines 287-332) Bloomfield provides what might be called an archetypal image of shared 'Plenty', which operates as a definitive if implied rebuke to the distinction between rich and poor of the Metropolis.

But it then turns out that 'Distinction' has now infested the country. For the vision Bloomfield has summoned up he consigns to 'days long past' (l. 333). Now, 'refinement' has left the peasant 'distanc'd in the mad'ning race' (ll. 337, 336). The social plan, 'that rank cements, as man to man' (l. 342), has been swept away by new considerations of rank, new forms of separation. As a result, 'Wealth flows around him, Fashion lordly reigns / Yet poverty is his, and mental pains' (ll. 343-4). Once the matter is put in those terms it must seem that the country and city are part of a social continuum rather than being distinguishable by the greater naturalness or morally sanctioned bonding between classes of the former. And to say this brings me to the question of Bloomfield's politics.

There can be no doubt that for the most part Bloomfield adopts that attitude towards rural circumstance which can be called conservative or which at all events sees in mutuality the 'cement' which holds the ranks together. During the 1780s, when he was working in London, he and his brother would go to hear Joseph Fawcett preach. Fawcett, a unitarian minister, used his Meeting House to lecture his audience, among whom were Wordsworth and Coleridge, on issues of the day, including the need for common ownership of the land. Robert Bloomfield was apparently much struck by Fawcett, yet it does not appear that his views were greatly modified by Fawcett's radicalism. Or should we see in his typical setting of poems in the past an implicit contrast with the unsatisfactory present? Perhaps. For, as I have previously noted, when Bloomfield writes about the present he tends to compare it unfavourably with the past. Yet he rarely links his criticisms of rank and new wealth to the grabbing of land. When, for example, he tells of Giles's work as shepherd, in 'Spring', he reports:

> Small was his charge: no wilds had they to roam;
> But bright inclosures circling round their home. (ll. 285-6)

By 'bright inclosures' I assume Bloomfield has in mind variegated hedgerows inside which the sheep are 'roving, ever seeking thee / Enchanting spirit, dear Variety!' ('Spring', ll. 289-90) This is a long way from Clare's view of enclosure. For him, it was 'vile', and so far from tolerating let alone encouraging, variety, it testified to the dread uniformity of 'little minds' which between them obliterated the divine 'glow' of nature. No brightness there—or indeed in Bloomfield's own prose 'Anecdotes and Observations', published after his death:

> Inclosing Acts! I do not much like the rage for them. They cut down the solemn, the venerable tree, and *sometimes* plant another,— not *always*; like a mercenary soldier, who kills more than he begets. (*Remains*, II, pp. 53-4)

We might wonder, though, why Clare so delighted in Bloomfield's work, why he was so sure that the older poet was indeed the English Theocritus. The answer is twofold. One, Bloomfield was writing about rural circumstance before enclosure had done its vilest work, or at all events Clare could think of him as doing so. It's true that on at least one occasion Bloomfield slips into the rhetoric we more usually associate with Clare. In his tale 'The Broken Crutch', a particular favourite of Clare's which appeared in the collection *Wild Flowers* (1806), the narrator savages:

This scythe of desolation call'd 'Reform'...
I hate the murderous axe; estranging more
The winding vale from what it was of yore,
Than e'en mortality in all its rage,
And all the change of faces in an age.
'Warmth', will they term it, that I speak so free;
They strip thy shades, thy shades so dear to me!
In Herbert's days woods cloth'd both hill and dale;
But peace, Remembrance! let us tell the tale. (ll. 68, 71-8)

Radstock called Clare's attack on enclosure 'radical slang'. He might well have applied the same phrase to Bloomfield's 'warmth', even though Bloomfield doesn't go so far as to identify who 'they' are who wield the murderous axe. Nor am I clear what he means by 'Reform'. What is clear is that Bloomfield is outraged by the licensed vandalism of those who destroy the look of his native place.

But this moment is remarkable because it is so unlike Bloomfield's usual procedure of focussing on a past which he regards with unabashed delight and yet which is never celebrated in a manner either condescending or belittling. This has especial point for both *Rural Tales* (1802) and *Wild Flowers*. Take for example one of the best known of the *Tales*, and one in which Clare particularly delighted. 'Richard and Kate; or Fair-Day, a Suffolk Ballad' can hardly be thought of as a grainily realistic account of rural life. Apart from anything else, the chances of the average couple in rural work reaching a hale and hearty old age, of all their children growing to adulthood, and of all of them marrying and producing their own full complement of healthy children, are slight. Crabbe was nearer the truth of the matter when, in *The Village*, he asked the sentimental townee in search of the picturesque to imagine life within the aesthetically pleasing cottage:

Go, if the peaceful cot your praises share,
Go look within, and ask if peace be there;
If peace be his—that drooping weary sire,
Or theirs, that offspring round their feeble fire;
Or hers, that matron pale, whose trembling hand
Turns on the wretched hearth th'expiring brand!

This might well be claimed for Theocritean realism: an immediate transcript of nature. But then it could be argued—and in a sense Clare does argue—that Crabbe's desire to dissolve the sentimental evasions of the picturesque lead him into his own evasions.[9] His villagers aren't allowed to speak. He speaks for them. And he presents them as objects of at best pity. Their lives are apparently entirely circumscribed and conditioned by work and their lousy living conditions. Yet after all Fair Days are an intrinsic part of the functioning rituals of rural life. And in Bloomfield's poem the ritual is made intrinsic to the lives of those who speak the poem—Richard and Kate, whose Suffolk dialect is sharply distinguished from that of the 'polite' narrator, with his reliance on what might be called 'literary' language. ('Kate scorn'd to damp the generous flame / That warm'd her aged Partner's breast').

'Richard and Kate' is, as the title of the volume in which it appears makes plain, a 'rural tale'. Wordsworth calls his great poem 'Michael' a Tale, and also a 'history / Homely and rude'. In his *Dictionary*, Johnson gives as the prime meaning of Tale: 'A narrative; a story. Commonly a slight or petty account of some trifling or fabulous incident.' And as a second definition, he offers 'Oral relation'. 'Tale' is thus identified with what for want of a better phrase I will call folk culture. Johnson's near contempt for such culture can be felt in his regarding tales as 'slight' and 'petty'; and as he quotes Macbeth's 'tale / Told by an idiot' it may be that he feels tales find a natural home in the society of country bumpkins. (Of *The Winter's Tale* he remarks in his *Notes to Shakespeare's Plays* that it is 'with all its absurdities, very entertaining'.) That Wordsworth was aware of this sense of tales as unworthy of 'high' culture is plain from his apparently defensive remark about the tale of Michael, that '*although* it be a history / Homely and rude, I will relate the same / For the delight of a few natural hearts' (my italics). 'Natural hearts': so much for those who can see little merit in a tale.

Tale telling is deeply inwoven into cultures where the printed word does not predominate. 'Blue-foot travellers' is the phrase reserved in the West Indian islands for those who have come some way in order to tell their tales and who are thus accorded especial hospitality. In the West of Ireland, as in rural Greece, a chair is still kept for the wanderer who may appear and who will bring with him a stock of tales to delight the household and any others who are called in to form the body of listeners. Such tales may well seem to deal in the 'trifling or fabulous'. It could be said that Bloomfield's 'The Fakenham Ghost' deals in both. But it also could and should be said that his *Rural Tales*—both in the volume that bears that name and elsewhere—draw on a cultural heritage whose riches lie in their being rooted, as ballads are, in material which is endlessly repeatable and thus shareable. This is the oral tradition. Moreover, as many of them are 'histories' of local people and places they make a community known to itself: they give it identity. Such identity is bound up with names of people, of places, of incidents, and, it should go without saying, of speech habits, idiom, of the real language of men.

As Dickens and Joyce above all should remind us, city culture can sustain tales quite as well as rural culture. But at the end of the eighteenth century most cities were new. Rural life, on the other hand, was old but changing, and the changes were coming with increased rapidity and for many were experienced as deeply disturbing. Time's alteration included the obliteration of what was nevertheless the tangible past. Tales were a means of sustaining a past which in all other ways had vanished. 'Where does the present go when it becomes the past?' Wittgenstein asked. Into tales is one answer. Hence, I suspect, the renewed interest in narrative poetry shown in our own day by such Australian poets as Philip Hodgins and Les Murray, both of them writing from rural circumstance. Hence, too, the narrative poems of the American poets David Mason and Andrew Hudgins, who want to reconstitute or, it may be more accurate to say, preserve a sense of their local culture, its social history, as existing beyond the metropolis.

Tales can of course degenerate into sentimental impositions on the actualities of history: bush ballads and cowboy poems are today's equivalents of much fake-ballad poetry of the late eighteenth and early nineteenth centuries (The kind Dickens has in mind in *Bleak House* when he causes Skimpole, who loves the 'artless', to sing of a poor country boy condemn'd to roam). This is not, however, an accusation that can be fairly levelled at Bloomfield. I don't even think he can be accused of having written with an eye to the main chance in *Good Tidings: or, News from The Farm*, his poem praising Jenner's discovery of vaccination against smallpox (1804), or in *The Banks of Wye* (1811). The former isn't hanging onto the coat-tails of Erasmus Darwin, who had undoubtedly popularised scientific subject-matter as material for poetry, but who has nothing of Bloomfield's concern with the horrors of disease. Darwin is an enlightenment poet. In his writings, Nature unfolds its great plan. For Bloomfield, on the other hand, the horrors of smallpox aren't to be softened by thoughts of an ultimately benevolent deity. As to *The Banks of Wye*, while I wouldn't disagree with John Barrell when he calls it a 'picturesque poem,' it should be noted that Bloomfield handles with both suppleness and ease the octosyllabic couplets he probably inherited from Dyer's poem *Grongar Hill* (1726), which had established a kind of template for future topographical cum picturesque poems.

This is perhaps the appropriate moment to remark that Bloomfield is technically adroit in handling a wide variety of verse forms, from the narrative couplets of *The Farmer's Boy*, through the intricate stanza patterns of 'The Widow to her Hour-Glass', ballad measures, sonnets, songs (also intricately patterned), to the unrhymed pentameters of 'To a Spindle'. This last, together with 'To My Old Oak Table', exhibits Bloomfield's assured handling of what Wordsworth would call 'domestic affections'. I doubt, however, that Wordsworth was in any sense a source for these fine poems.[10] Cowper is a far more likely influence. Although there are precedents for his 'On the Receipt of my Mother's Picture out of Norfolk, the gift of my Cousin, Ann Bodham',[11] Cowper's is undoubtedly a new kind of meditative poem, in which memory called up by an object testifies to the deep emotional bonding between the object's original owner—friend, relative—and the poet who now contemplates it. Wordsworth learnt from Cowper in this respect and so, too, did Clare, although in Clare's case the friend or relative is usually the land itself, and the land's one-time ownership of, say, Swordy Well or Langley Bush, prompts memories that lead both to elegy and to poems of bitter protest over lost possessions.

Despite Bloomfield's recording his mother's fear of 'Winter, Old Age, and Poverty', his poem is in no sense one of protest. Her life and death are gathered into a measured statement which is almost a memento mori:

> —Half finish'd? 'Tis the motto of the world!
> We spin vain threads, and strive, and die
> With sillier things than spindles on our hands! (ll. 26-7)

'To a Spindle' is a triumph of what Donald Davie memorably called 'the chastity of poetic diction'. Its restraint and economy of metaphor establish a tone of scrupulous regard for its subject—which is ultimately with how to live a life of good intent. And if this makes the poem sound at all pietistic I need to add that its sweetness has nothing at all to do with pietism. The same may be said of 'To My Old Oak Table', in which the loving, intimate familiarity of address, of murmuring, sounds a note which is to my ear at least quite new in English poetry, although it is one which will be picked up and adapted by Clare, in for example 'To A Fallen Elm', and, later, by Thomas Hardy. These two poems of Bloomfield's are of unique accomplishment and value. That they should be absent from virtually all anthologies of poetry of the period is quite simply a scandal.

The same holds true of *May-Day with the Muses*. This was Bloomfield's last substantial work, published in 1822, the year before he died, and written at a time of personal distress. He was physically in poor shape, and as his wife seems to have given most of his by no means considerable income into the unsafe keeping of Joanna Southcott's followers, Bloomfield had been reduced to near poverty. This may be why the poem has an elegiac feel about it. The community with which it deals is not so much set in the past as consigned to it. In this, it seems to develop out of 'The Broken Crutch', a tale about a marriage between a gentleman of honour and a poor girl which is very pointedly set in what is made to feel an already remote moment of social history, even though it is within living memory of the narrator. 'The moat remains; the dwelling is no more! / Its name denotes its melancholy fall, / For village children call the spot "Burnt-Hall"'. So we are told of the hall to which Herbert Brooks, the hero of 'The Broken Crutch' brings Peggy, his wife. What we don't however know is why the hall was burnt. An accident? Because Brooks' fortune had gone? Is this the work of nature or of man?[12]

In *May-Day with the Muses* we meet Sir Ambrose Higham, owner of Oakly Hall, 'in his eightieth year', who honours the muses and who has, we are told, found sparks of genius 'In many a local ballad, many a tale, / As wild and brief as cowslips in the dale, / Though unrecorded as the gleams of light / That vanish in the quietness of night.' His sudden decision to allow his tenants to 'pay their rents in rhyme' therefore provides Bloomfield with a device to record a number of 'local tales'. *May-Day with the Muses* is taken up with tales in rhyme delivered by Sir Ambrose's tenants at the Hall's May Day celebrations. I can find no evidence that Tennyson knew Bloomfield's poems, but I am reasonably sure he must have done so. It is difficult not to think that works such as *The Princess*, which Tennyson called 'A Medley', and the *English Idyls* find a starting point in Bloomfield's own medley. *May-Day with the Muses* is in this sense original.

It is also constrained by the nipping air of Evangelicalism, and perhaps by Bloomfield's sensitivity to his wife's religious allegiances. (Joanna Southcott was an ardent Methodist.) Sir Ambrose proposes to outlaw certain tales. He wants 'No stupid ghost, no vulgar thing', nor should tales 'brood o'er midnight darkness, crimes, and blood.' This is surely a sanitised version of cottage tales? To account for why this might be, we should recall that the Society for the Suppression of Vice, which had been set up by the Evangelicals, was busy prosecuting bookshops that stored material of which it disapproved. (In 1822 the Society, of which Clare's patron, Lord Radstock, was Vice-President, managed to have Richard Carlile thrown into prison for selling *Queen Mab*.) We should also note that the first tale to be told at Oakly Hall is of 'The Drunken Father', and that by the time Bloomfield came to write and publish *May-Day with the Muses* Evangelicalism had taken up the cause of temperance with an especial vigour. (Although Bloomfield allows the 'mouldy barrel' brought in for the celebrations to be drained.) Other tales, including the forester's, plead the cause of quietism, of contentment with your lot, which is essential to Evangelicalism's vision of the good society.

If none of this seems to overset the achievement of Bloomfield's work, it is, I think, because we are able to see *May-Day with the Muses* as an idyll in the sense of 'any scene of tranquil happiness.' And 'idyllic', which had come into use in the early eighteenth century, although Johnson does not give it, commonly means 'a serene and euphoric state or environment which is remotely attainable and idealised'. Bloomfield himself describes the scene at Oakly Hall as one 'that Wilkie might have touch'd with pride'. David Wilkie (1785-1841) who had gained his A.R.A. in 1809, the earliest the honour could be conferred on him, was by the 1820s the most popular genre painter of his day. Works such as 'The Blind Fiddler', 'Card Players', 'Reading the Will,' 'The Village Festival' and 'The Rent Day', were much copied, reproduced and imitated. Wilkie's studies of rural circumstance soften harsh realities by a suggestion of the quaint. We might say that *May-Day with the Muses* does something very similar. But Bloomfield escapes the charge of evasiveness that this implies, just as Keats escapes the charge that in his great semi-Georgic poem 'To Autumn' he idealises what in 1819 was a particularly brutal autumn, as the events at Peterloo made all-too plain. *May-Day with the Muses* offers a vision of rural circumstance which, the poem acknowledges, is ideal, and to be found, if anywhere, only in the past. And its close, the re-enactment of marriage vows between Sir Ambrose and his aged wife, at once celebrates their enduring love and acknowledges its inevitable ending. The last lines of the poem run:

> Nor was the lawn clear till the moon arose,
> And on each turret pour'd a brilliant gleam
> Of modest light, that trembled on the stream;
> The owl awoke, but dared not yet complain,
> And banish'd silence re-assumed her reign.
> ['The end of the competition', ll. 110-14]

Moonlight, turrets, the solitary owl. Picturesque properties, emblems of 'the principle of change' in which the picturesque deals and which, as a result, denies that human agency is in any sense implicated in, or could be responsible for, such change.[13] Yet Bloomfield's surely deliberate echo of a famous line of Pope at the very end of his poem suggests he is fully aware of Time's Alteration. In his Fourth Moral Essay Pope had foreseen the fall of pride, of new wealth, grandeur, and the restoration to the land of health and fruitfulness. And so, contemplating the beggaring of a man whom most commentators take to be the Duke of Chandos and the pulling down of his great house, Cannons, Pope sees 'Deep Harvests bury all his Pride has planned, / And laughing Ceres reassume the Land'. By substituting 'banish'd Silence' for 'laughing Ceres', Bloomfield hints at an ending far from Pope's intent. Laughing Ceres beautifully allows for the idea of renewed festival, of harvest as a time of communality. But the Mayday celebrations Bloomfield attends to are, he knows, done with. Hence, I think, the ground bass of the poem, its strongly elegiac note. 'Such scenes were England's boast in days gone by,' the poem's narrator at one point remarks of Oakly Hall's Mayday celebrations. Now, only art can preserve them. Bloomfield acknowledges as much when he says that had Wilkie painted the scene at Oakly Hall, 'The May-day banquet then had never died.' Now, it can live only through his poem, just as 'local tales' can live only through—the ballads and poems made for Sir Ambrose by his tenants. And Sir Ambrose's response to those tales is therefore crucial. He tells them:

> Your verses shall not die as heretofore;
> Your local tales shall not be thrown away...
> I purpose then to send them forth to try
> The public patience, or its apathy.
> The world shall see them; why should I refrain?
> 'Tis all the produce of my own domain.
>   ['The end of the competition', ll. 80-81, 87-90]

This may be compared with Wordsworth's expressed purpose at the opening of 'Michael' to preserve the history 'homely and rude':

> For the delight of a few natural hearts,
> And with yet fonder feeling, for the sake
> Of youthful Poets, who among these Hills
> Will be my second self when I am gone.

With the possible exception of Norman Nicholson in this century, Wordsworth had no second self. Bloomfield, however, did. His abiding concern for local tales was shared by his 'brother bard and fellow labourer', John Clare. For them all, the vast changes being enacted across the country became matter for poetry. And if Wordsworth spoke for them all when he claimed the poet's responsibility to preserve 'things silently gone out of mind and things violently destroyed,' they speak for him in providing poetic testimony of the real language of men and of the incidents of common life made interesting. Which is one way of saying that we cannot hope properly to understand that historical period which is habitually called Romanticism if we do not pay attention to the works of Robert Bloomfield.

John Lucas

Footnotes
1. Bloomfield continued to sell remarkably well, however, until quite late in the century. See the statistics on his sales compiled by B.C. Bloomfield in 'The Publication of *The Farmer's Boy*,' *The Library*, 6th ser., 15, no. 2 (June 1993), 75-94, pp. 91-3.
2. Edward Thomas, 'W.H. Hudson' in *A Language Not To Be Betrayed: Selected Prose of Edward Thomas*, ed. Edna Longley (Manchester: Carcanet, 1981), p. 143. In her Index Longley identifies Bloomfield as 'Roger Bloomfield', evidence of how deeply neglect of the poet has reached.
3. Edward Young, 'Conjectures on Original Composition.' The essay, which was first written in 1759, became a key point of reference for those seeking to overthrow the influence of Pope and his school of neo-classical writers. For more on this see my *England and Englishness: Ideas of Nationhood in English Poetry 1688-1900* (London: Hogarth Press, 1990), pp. 50-3.
4. From the second edition, 1692, vol. 2, p. 6.
5. See my essay 'Bloomfield and Clare' in *The Independent Spirit: John Clare and the Self-taught Tradition*, ed. John Goodridge, (Helpston: The John Clare Society and the Margaret Grainger Memorial Trust, 1994), esp. pp. 61-4.
6. British Library, Add. MS 28268, f. 351, quoted by J.N. Lawson, in his *Collected Poems by Robert Bloomfield* (Gainesville, Florida: Scholars' Facsimiles and Reprints, 1971), p. xii.
7. John Barrell, *The Idea of Landscape and the Sense of Place, 1730- 1840: an Approach to the Poetry of John Clare* (London: Cambridge University Press,

1972), p. 225.
8. Barrell, p. 126.
9. I think in particular of Clare's remark that compared to Bloomfield, 'Crabbe writes about the peasantry as much like the Magistrate as the Poet. He is determined to show you their worst side...' (Clare to Allan Cunningham, 9 September 1824, quoted in *John Clare: Cottage Tales*, ed. Eric Robinson, David Powell and P.M.S. Dawson (Manchester: Carcanet, 1993), p. ix.
10. Bloomfield knew and admired *Lyrical Ballads*, however: see *Remains*, II, pp. 111, 119.
11. See the chapter on this in Vincent Newey, *Cowper's Poetry: A Critical Study and Reassessment* (Liverpool: Liverpool University Press, 1982), pp. 245-70.
12. For the origin of Bloomfield's tale see the story about the Countess of Exeter in the *Monthly Magazine*, March 1797, reprinted in *Cottage Tales*, op. cit., pp. 135-7.
13. For the properties and politics of the picturesque see my essay 'Places and Dwellings: Wordsworth, Clare and the anti-picturesque', in *The Iconography of Landscape*, eds. Denis Cosgrove and Stephen Daniels (Cambridge: Cambridge University Press, 1988), pp. 33-97.

Further Reading

Editions

Bloomfield's collected poems were reprinted many times in the nineteenth-century, and it is still possible to find second-hand copies of these editions, as well as of the single works (most of which also went through many editions). Modern editions have been very much less frequent, and the major ones are listed here (including facsimile reprints) in chronological order. The Gregg and Lark editions are still in print.

The Farmer's Boy (London: Staples Books, 1941).
A Selection of Poems by Robert Bloomfield, edited with an Introduction by Roland Gant (London: The Grey Walls Press, 1947).
Selections from the Correspondence of Robert Bloomfield, ed. W. H. Hart (London: Spottiswoode, 1870, privately reprinted by Robert F. Ashby, 1968).
Collected Poems (1800-1822), ed. J. N. Lawson, five volumes in one (Gainesville: Scholars' Facsimiles and Reprints, 1971).
The Farmer's Boy: The Story of a Suffolk Poet, Robert Bloomfield, His Life and Poems 1766-1823, ed. William Wickett and Nicholas Duval (Lavenham: Terence Dalton, 1971), a selected edition and biography.
The Poems of Robert Bloomfield [1827], facsimile (Farnborough: Gregg International, 1971).
Wild Flowers, The Banks of Wye, and May Day with the Muses, introduced by D. H. Reiman (New York and London: Garland, 1977).
The Farmer's Boy (Bury St. Edmunds: Lark Books, 1986).

Biographical and Critical

This is largely confined to modern work, with three examples of the nineteenth-century response. Again, the listing is chronological.

E.W. Brayley, *Views in Suffolk, Norfolk and Northamptonshire, illustrative of the Works of Robert Bloomfield* (London: Vernor, Hood and others, 1806).
Spencer T. Hall, 'Bloomfield and Clare', in his *Biographical Sketches of Remarkable People, Chiefly from Personal Recollection; with Miscellaneous Papers and Poems* (London: Simpkin, Marshall and Co., 1873).

W.E. Wink, *Lives of the Illustrious Shoemakers* (London: Sampson Low and others, 1883), pp. 100-116.

A.H.R. Fairchild, 'Robert Bloomfield', *Studies in Philology*, 16 (1919).

Edmund Blunden, *Nature in English Literature* (1929; reprinted New York: Kennikat Press, 1970), Chapter 5 (on Stephen Duck and Bloomfield).

Rayner Unwin, *The Rural Muse* (London: George Allen and Unwin, 1954), pp. 87-120.

Graham F. Reed, 'Bloomfield's Aeolus', *Notes and Queries*, 201 (Oct 1956), 450-1.

The Earl of Cranbrook and John Hadfield, 'Some Uncollected Authors XX: Robert Bloomfield 1766-1823', *Book Collector*, 8 (1959), 170-9, 299, 431-2.

A.J. Sambrook, 'The Farmer's Boy: Robert Bloomfield, 1766-1823', *English*, 16 (1967), 167-71.

H.H. Bloomfield, 'The Robert Bloomfield Bicentenary', *Bedfordshire Magazine*, Vol. 10, no. 80 (Spring 1967).

Jonathan Lawson, *Robert Bloomfield* (Boston: G. K. Hall, 1980). Twayne's English Authors Series, no. 310.

Robert F. Ashby, 'The First Editions of *The Farmer's Boy*', *Book Collector*, 41, part 2 (1992), 180-7.

B.C. Bloomfield, 'The Publication of *The Farmer's Boy*', *The Library*, 6th ser., 15, no. 2 (June 1993), 75-94.

John Lucas, 'Bloomfield and Clare', in *The Independent Spirit: John Clare and the Self-Taught Tradition*, ed. John Goodridge (Helpston: The John Clare Society and the Margaret Grainger Memorial Trust, 1994), pp. 55-68 (see also Ronald Blythe's remarks on Bloomfield, pp. 181-4).

Annette Wheeler Cafarelli, 'The Romantic "Peasant" Poets and their Patrons', *The Wordsworth Circle*, 26 (1995), 77-87 (reads Bloomfield as a 'transforming presence' in the history of peasant poetry).

Tim Fulford and Beth Lee, 'The Jenneration of Disease: Vaccination, Romanticism and Revolution', forthcoming (includes discussion of *Good Tidings*).

The Farmer's Boy (1800)

From the Preface to Poems (1809), Volume II [Bloomfield quotes a letter to his brother George Bloomfield, which accompanied the manuscript of the poem]

London, Sunday, Sept. 16, 1798

Dear George,

I gave you a hint long ago that I was making rhymes. I now send the Poem, as a present to my Mother. It coming through your hands, you will be at liberty to detain it as long as you please; and I have no doubt but some parts of it will please you. I would wish you to observe well the following remarks, and I wish you to be candid if it should ever draw any remarks from you.

When I began it, I thought to myself that I could complete it in a twelvemonth, allowing myself three months for each quarter; but I soon found that I could not; and indeed I made it longer than I at first intended.* Nine tenths of it were put together as I sat at work, where there are usually six of us. No one in the house has any knowledge of what I have employed my thoughts about when I did not talk.

I chose to do it in rhime for this reason; because I found always that when I put two or three lines together in blank verse, or something that sounded like it, it was ten to one if it stood right when it came to be written down. Winter and half of Autumn were done long before I could find leisure to write them. In the 'Harvest Home' you will find the essence of letters which you wrote formerly to London.

When I had nearly done it, it came strongly into my mind that very silly things are sometimes printed; but by what means I knew not. To try and get at this knowledge, I resolved to make some efforts of the sort; and what encouraged me to go through with it was, that, if I got laughed at, no one that I cared for could know it, unless I myself told them...

* The parts of the poem first composed, before any thought was entertained of going through with the Seasons, were the morning scene in Spring, beginning 'This task had *Giles*,' and the description of the lambs at play. And if it be lawful for an author to tell his opinion, they have never lost an inch of ground in my estimation from that day to this.

SPRING. I

Argument. Invocation, &c. Seed time. Harrowing. Morning walks. Milking. The Dairy. Suffolk Cheese. Spring coming forth. Sheep fond of changing. Lambs at play. The Butcher, &c.

O Come, blest Spirit! whatsoe'er thou art,
Thou kindling warmth that hover'st round my heart,
Sweet inmate, hail! thou source of sterling joy,
That poverty itself cannot destroy,
Be thou my Muse; and faithful still to me,
Retrace the paths of wild obscurity.
No deeds of arms my humble lines rehearse;
No Alpine wonders thunder through my verse,
The roaring cataract, the snow-topt hill,
Inspiring awe, till breath itself stands still: 10
Nature's sublimer scenes ne'er charm'd mine eyes,
Nor Science led me through the boundless skies;
From meaner objects far my raptures flow:
O point these raptures! bid my bosom glow!
And lead my soul to ecstasies of praise
For all the blessings of my infant days!
Bear me through regions where gay Fancy dwells;
But mould to Truth's fair form what Memory tells.
    Live, trifling incidents, and grace my song,

That to the humblest menial belong: 20
To him whose drudgery unheeded goes,
His joys unreckon'd as his cares or woes;
Though joys and cares in every path are sown,
And youthful minds have feelings of their own,
Quick springing sorrows, transient as the dew,
Delights from trifles, trifles ever new.
'Twas thus with Giles: meek, fatherless and poor;
Labour his portion, but he felt no more;
No stripes, no tyranny his steps pursu'd;
His life was constant, cheerful servitude: 30
Strange to the world, he wore a bashful look,
The fields his study, Nature was his book;
And, as revolving Seasons chang'd the scene
From heat to cold, tempestuous to serene,
Though every change still varied his employ,
Yet each new duty brought its share of joy.
    Where noble Grafton spreads his rich domains,
Round Euston's water'd vale, and sloping plains,
Where woods and groves in solemn grandeur rise,
Where the kite brooding unmolested flies;   40
The woodcock and the painted pheasant race,
And sculking Foxes, destin'd for the chace;
There Giles, untaught and unrepining, stray'd
Through every copse, and grove, and winding glade;
There his first thoughts to Nature's charms inclin'd,
That stamps devotion on th'inquiring mind.
A little farm his generous Master till'd,
Who with peculiar grace his station fill'd;
By deeds of hospitality endear'd,
Serv'd from affection, for his worth rever'd;   50
A happy offspring blest his plenteous board,
His fields were fruitful, and his barns well stor'd.
And fourscore ewes he fed, a sturdy team,
And lowing kine that graz'd beside the stream:
Unceasing industry he kept in view;
And never lack'd a job for Giles to do.
    Fled now the sullen murmurs of the North,
The splendid raiment of the Spring peeps forth;
Her universal green, and the clear sky,

Delight still more and more the gazing eye.   60
Wide o'er the fields, in rising moisture strong,
Shoots up the simple flower, or creeps along
The mellow'd soil; imbibing fairer hues,
Or sweets from frequent showers and evening dews;
That summon from their sheds the slumb'ring plows,
While health impregnates every breeze that blows.
No wheels support the diving, pointed, share;
No groaning ox is doom'd to labour there;
No helpmates teach the docile steed his road;
(Alike unknown the ploughboy and the goad;)   70
But, unassisted through each toilsome day,
With smiling brow the plowman cleaves his way,
Draws his fresh parallels, and, wid'ning still,
Treads slow the heavy dale, or climbs the hill:
Strong on the wing his busy followers play,
Where writhing earth-worms meet th'unwelcome day;
Till all is chang'd, and hill and level down
Assume a livery of sober brown:
Again disturb'd, when Giles with wearying strides
From ridge to ridge the ponderous harrow guides;   80
His heels deep sinking every step he goes,
Till dirt adhesive loads his clouted shoes.
Welcome green headland! firm beneath his feet;
Welcome the friendly bank's refreshing seat;
There, warm with toil, his panting horses browse
Their shelt'ring canopy of pendent boughs;
Till rest, delicious, chase each transient pain,
And new-born vigour swell in every vein.
Hour after hour, and day to day succeeds;
Till every clod and deep-drawn furrow spreads   90
To crumbling mould; a level surface clear,
And strew'd with corn to crown the rising year;
And o'er the whole Giles once transverse again,
In earth's moist bosom buries up the grain.
The work is done; no more to man is given;
The grateful Farmer trusts the rest to Heaven.
Yet oft with anxious heart he looks around,
And marks the first green blade that breaks the ground;
In fancy sees his trembling oats uprun,

His tufted barley yellow with the sun;   100
Sees clouds propitious shed their timely store,
And all his harvest gather'd round his door.
But still unsafe the big swoln grain below,
A fav'rite morsel with the Rook and Crow;
From field to field the flock increasing goes;
To level crops most formidable foes:
Their danger well the wary plunderers know,
And place a watch on some conspicuous bough;
Yet oft the sculking gunner by surprise
Will scatter death amongst them as they rise.   110
These, hung in triumph round the spacious field,
At best will but a short-liv'd terror yield:
Nor guards of property; (not penal law,
But harmless riflemen of rags and straw;)
Familiariz'd to these, they boldly rove,
Nor heed such sentinels that never move.
Let then your birds lie prostrate on the earth,
In dying posture, and with wings stretcht forth;
Shift them at eve or morn from place to place,
And Death shall terrify the pilfering race;   120
In the mid air, while circling round and round,
They call their lifeless comrades from the ground;
With quick'ning wing, and notes of loud alarm,
Warn the whole flock to shun th'impending harm.
     This task had Giles, in fields remote from home:
Oft has he wish'd the rosy morn to come:
Yet never fam'd was he nor foremost found
To break the seal of sleep; his sleep was sound:
But when at day-break summon'd from his bed,
Light as the lark that carol'd o'er his head.—   130
His sandy way, deep-worn by hasty showers,
O'er-arch'd with oaks that form'd fantastic bow'rs,
Waving aloft their tow'ring branches proud,
In borrow'd tinges from the eastern cloud,
Gave inspiration, pure as ever flow'd,
And genuine transport in his bosom glow'd.
His own shrill matin join'd the various notes
Of Nature's music, from a thousand throats:
The Blackbird strove with emulation sweet,

And Echo answer'd from her close retreat;   140
The sporting White-throat on some twig's end borne,
Pour'd hymns to freedom and the rising morn;
Stopt in her song perchance the starting Thrush
Shook a white shower from the black-thorn bush,
Where dew-drops thick as early blossoms hung,
And trembled as the minstrel sweetly sung.
Across his path, in either grove to hide,
The timid Rabbit scouted by his side;
Or Pheasant boldly stalk'd along the road,
Whose gold and purple tints alternate glow'd.   150
    But groves no farther fenc'd the devious way;
A wide-extended heath before him lay,
Where on the grass the stagnant shower had run,
And shone a mirror to the rising sun,
Thus doubly seen to light a distant wood,
To give new life to each expanding bud;
And chase away the dewy foot-marks found,
Where prowling Reynard trod his nightly round;
To shun whose thefts 'twas Giles's evening care,
His feather'd victims to suspend in air,   160
High on the bough that nodded o'er his head,
And thus each morn to strew the field with dead.
    His simple errand done, he homeward hies;
Another instantly its place supplies.
The clatt'ring Dairy-Maid immers'd in steam,
Singing and scrubbing midst her milk and cream,
Bawls out, 'Go fetch the Cows!' ...he hears no more;
For pigs, and ducks, and turkies, throng the door,
And sitting hens, for constant war prepar'd;
A concert strange to that which late he heard.   170
Straight to the meadow then he whistling goes;
With well-known halloo calls his lazy Cows:
Down the rich pasture heedlessly they graze,
Or hear the summons with an idle gaze;
For well they know the cow-yard yields no more
Its tempting fragrance, nor its wintry store.
Reluctance marks their steps, sedate and slow;
The right of conquest all the law they know:
The strong press on, the weak by turns succeed,

And one superior always takes the lead;   180
Is ever foremost, wheresoe'er they stray:
Allow'd precedence, undisputed sway:
With jealous pride her station is maintain'd,
For many a broil that post of honour gain'd.
At home, the yard affords a grateful scene;
For Spring makes e'en a miry cow-yard clean.
Thence from its chalky bed behold convey'd
The rich manure that drenching Winter made,
Which pil'd near home, grows green with many a weed,
A promis'd nutriment for Autumn's seed.   190
Forth comes the Maid, and like the morning smiles;
The Mistress too, and follow'd close by Giles.
A friendly tripod forms their humble seat,
With pails bright scour'd, and delicately sweet.
Where shadowing elms obstruct the morning ray,
Begins the work, begins the simple lay;
The full charg'd udder yields its willing streams,
While Mary sings some lover's amorous dreams;
And crouching Giles beneath a neighbouring tree
Tugs o'er his pail, and chants with equal glee;   200
Whose hat with tatter'd brim, of nap so bare,
From the cow's side purloins a coat of hair,
A mottled ensign of his harmless trade,
An unambitious, peaceable cockade.
As unambitious too that cheerful aid
The Mistress yields beside her rosy Maid;
With joy she views her plenteous reeking store,
And bears a brimmer to the dairy door;
Her Cows dismiss'd, the luscious mead to roam,
Till eve again recall them loaded home.   210
And now the Dairy claims her choicest care,
And half her household find employment there:
Slow rolls the churn, its load of clogging cream
At once foregoes its quality and name;
From knotty particles first floating wide
Congealing butter's dash'd from side to side;
Streams of new milk through flowing coolers stray,
And snow-white curd abounds, and wholesome whey.
Due north th'unglazed windows, cold and clear,

For warming sunbeams are unwelcome here.   220
Brisk goes the work beneath each busy hand,
And Giles must trudge, whoever gives command;
A Gibeonite, that serves them all by turns:
He drains the pump, from him the faggot burns;
From him the noisy Hogs demand their food;
While at his heels run many a chirping brood,
Or down his path in expectation stand,
With equal claims upon his strewing hand.
Thus wastes the morn, till each with pleasure sees
The bustle o'er, and press'd the new-made cheese.   230
    Unrivall'd stands thy country Cheese, O Giles!
Whose very name alone engenders smiles;
Whose fame abroad by every tongue is spoke,
The well-known butt of many a flinty joke,
That pass like current coin the nation through;
And, ah! experience proves the satire true.
Provision's grave, thou ever-craving mart,
Dependant, huge Metropolis! where Art
Her poring thousands stows in breathless rooms,
Midst pois'nous smokes, and steams, and rattling looms;   240
Where Grandeur revels in unbounded stores;
Restraint, a slighted stranger at their doors!
Thou, like a whirlpool, drain'st the countries round,
Till London market, London price, resound
Through every town, round every passing load,
And dairy produce throngs the eastern road:
Delicious veal, and butter, every hour,
From Essex lowlands, and the banks of Stour;
And further far, where numerous herds repose,
From Orwell's brink, from Waveny, or Ouse.   250
Hence Suffolk dairy-wives run mad for cream,
And leave their milk with nothing but its name;
Its name derision and reproach pursue,
And strangers tell of 'three times skimm'd sky-blue.'
To cheese converted, what can be its boast?
What, but the common virtues of a post!
If drought o'ertake it faster than the knife,
Most fair it bids for stubborn length of life,
And, like the oaken shelf whereon 'tis laid,

Mocks the weak efforts of the bending blade;   260
Or in the hog-trough rests in perfect spite,
Too big to swallow, and too hard to bite.
Inglorious victory! Ye Cheshire meads,
Or Severn's flow'ry dales, where Plenty treads,
Was your rich milk to suffer wrongs like these,
Farewell your pride! farewell renowned cheese!
The skimmer dread, whose ravages alone
Thus turn the mead's sweet nectar into stone.
     Neglected now the early daisy lies;
Nor thou, pale primrose, bloom'st the only prize: 270
Advancing Spring profusely spreads abroad
Flow'rs of all hues, with sweetest fragrance stor'd;
Where'er she treads, Love gladdens every plain,
Delight on tiptoe bears her lucid train;
Sweet Hope with conscious brow before her flies
Anticipating wealth from Summer skies;
All Nature feels her renovating sway;
The sheep-fed pasture, and the meadow gay
And trees, and shrubs, no longer budding seen
Display the new-grown branch of lighter green;   280
On airy downs the idling Shepherd lies,
And sees to-morrow in the marbled skies.
Here then, my soul, thy darling theme pursue,
For every day was Giles a Shepherd too.
     Small was his charge: no wilds had they to roam;
But bright inclosures circling round their home.
No yellow-blossomed furze, nor stubborn thorn,
The heath's rough produce, had their fleeces torn,
Yet ever roving, ever seeking thee,
Enchanting spirit, dear Variety!   290
O happy tenants, prisoners of a day!
Releas'd to ease, to pleasure, and to play;
Indulg'd through every field by turns to range,
And taste them all in one continual change.
For though luxuriant their grassy food,
Sheep long confin'd but loathe the present good;
Bleating around the homeward gate they meet,
And starve, and pine, with plenty at their feet.
Loos'd from the winding lane, a joyful throng,

See, o'er yon pasture, how they pour along!   300
Giles round their boundaries takes his usual stroll;
Sees every pass secur'd, and fences whole;
High fences, proud to charm the gazing eye,
Where many a nestling first assays to fly;
Where blows the woodbine, faintly streak'd with red,
And rests on every bough its tender head;
Round the young ash its twining branches meet,
Or crown the hawthorn with its odours sweet.
     Say, ye that know, ye who have felt and seen,
Spring's morning smiles, and soul-enliv'ning green,   310
Say, did you give the thrilling transport way?
Did your eye brighten, when young Lambs at play
Leap'd o'er your path with animated pride,
Or gaz'd in merry clusters by your side?
Ye who can smile, to wisdom no disgrace,
At the arch meaning of a Kitten's face:
If spotless innocence, and infant mirth,
Excites to praise, or gives reflection birth;
In shades like these pursue your fav'rite joy,
Midst Nature's revels, sports that never cloy.   320
     A few begin a short but vigorous race,
And Indolence abash'd soon flies the place;
Thus challeng'd forth, see thither one by one,
From every side assembling playmates run;
A thousand wily antics mark their stay,
A starting crowd, impatient of delay.
Like the fond dove, from fearful prison freed,
Each seems to say, 'Come, let us try our speed;'
Away they scour, impetuous, ardent, strong,
The green turf trembling as they bound along;   330
Adown the slope, then up the hillock climb,
Where every molehill is a bed of thyme;
There panting stop; yet scarcely can refrain;
A bird, a leaf, will set them off again:
Or, if a gale with strength unusual blow,
Scatt'ring the wild-briar roses into snow,
Their little limbs increasing efforts try,
Like the torn flower the fair assemblage fly.
Ah, fallen rose! sad emblem of their doom;

Frail as thyself, they perish while they bloom!   340
Though unoffending Innocence may plead,
Though frantic Ewes may mourn the savage deed,
Their shepherd comes, a messenger of blood,
And drives them bleating from their sports and food.
Care loads his brow, and pity wrings his heart,
For lo, the murd'ring Butcher, with his cart,
Demands the firstlings of his flock to die,
And makes a sport of life and liberty!
His gay companions Giles beholds no more;
Clos'd are their eyes, their fleeces drench'd in gore;   350
Nor can Compassion, with her softest notes,
Withhold the knife that plunges thro' their throats.
　　　Down, indignation! hence, ideas foul!
Away the shocking image from my soul!
Let kindlier visitants attend my way,
Beneath approaching Summer's fervid ray;
Nor thankless glooms obtrude, nor cares annoy,
Whilst the sweet theme is universal joy.

SUMMER. II

Argument. Turnip sowing. Wheat ripening. Sparrows. Insects. The sky-lark. Reaping, &c. Harvest-field, Dairymaid, &c. Labours of the barn. The gander. Night; a thunder-storm. Harvest-home. Reflections, &c.

The Farmer's life displays in every part
A moral lesson to the sensual heart.
Though in the lap of Plenty, thoughtful still,
He looks beyond the present good or ill;
Nor estimates alone one blessing's worth,
From changeful seasons, or capricious earth;
But views the future with the present hours,
And looks for failures as he looks for showers;
For casual as for certain want prepares,
And round his yard the reeking haystack rears;   10
Or clover, blossom'd lovely to the sight,
His team's rich store through many a wintry night.
What though abundance round his dwelling spreads,
Though ever moist his self-improving meads
Supply his dairy with a copious flood,
And seem to promise unexhausted food;
That promise fails, when buried deep in snow,
And vegetative juices cease to flow.
For this, his plough turns up the destin'd lands,

Whence stormy Winter draws its full demands;   20
For this, the seed minutely small, he sows,
Whence, sound and sweet, the hardy turnip grows.
But how unlike to April's closing days!
High climbs the Sun, and darts his powerful rays;
Whitens the fresh-drawn mould, and pierces through
The cumb'rous clods that tumble round the plough.
O'er heaven's bright azure hence with joyful eyes
The Farmer sees dark clouds assembling rise;
Borne o'er his fields a heavy torrent falls,
And strikes the earth in hasty driving squalls.   30
'Right welcome down, ye precious drops,' he cries;
But soon, too soon, the partial blessing flies.
'Boy, bring thy harrows! try how deep the rain
Has forced its way.' He comes, but comes in vain;
Dry dust beneath the bubbling surface lurks,
And mocks his pains the more, the more he works:
Still, midst huge clods, he plunges on forlorn,
That laugh his harrows and the shower to scorn.
E'en thus the living clod, the stubborn fool,
Resists the stormy lectures of the school,   40
Till tried with gentler means, the dunce to please,
His head imbibes right reason by degrees;
As when from eve till morning's wakeful hour,
Light, constant rain evinces secret pow'r,
And ere the day resumes its wonted smiles,
Presents a cheerful, easy task for Giles.
Down with a touch the mellow'd soil is laid,
And yon tall crop next claims his timely aid;
Thither well pleas'd he hies, assur'd to find
Wild, trackless haunts, and objects to his mind.   50
        Shot up from broad rank blades that droop below,
The nodding Wheat-ear forms a graceful bow,
With milky kernels starting full, weigh'd down,
Ere yet the sun hath ting'd its head with brown;
There thousands in a flock, for ever gay,
Loud chirping sparrows welcome on the day,
And from the mazes of the leafy thorn
Drop one by one upon the bending corn.
Giles with a pole assails their close retreats,

And round the grass grown dewy border beats,   60
On either side completely overspread,
Here branches bend, there corn o'ertops his head.
Green covert, hail! for through the varying year
No hours so sweet, no scene to him so dear.
Here Wisdom's placid eye delighted sees
His frequent intervals of lonely ease,
And with one ray his infant soul inspires,
Just kindling there her never-dying fires,
Whence solitude derives peculiar charms,
And heaven-directed thought his bosom warms.   70
Just where the parting bough's light shadows play,
Scarce in the shade, nor in the scorching day,
Stretch'd on the turf he lies, a peopled bed,
Where swarming insects creep around his head.
The small dust-colour'd beetle climbs with pain
O'er the smooth plantain-leaf, a spacious plain!
Thence higher still, by countless steps convey'd,
He gains the summit of a shiv'ring blade,
And flirts his filmy wings, and looks around,
Exulting in his distance from the ground.   80
The tender speckled moth here dancing seen,
The vaulting grasshopper of glossy green,
And all prolific Summer's sporting train,
Their little lives by various pow'rs sustain.
But what can unassisted vision do?
What, but recoil where most it would pursue;
His patient gaze but finish with a sigh,
When Music waking speaks the sky-lark nigh.
Just starting from the corn, he cheerly sings,
And trusts with conscious pride his downy wings;   90
Still louder breathes, and in the face of day
Mounts up, and calls on Giles to mark his way.
Close to his eyes his hat he instant bends,
And forms a friendly telescope, that lends
Just aid enough to dull the glaring light,
And place the wand'ring bird before his sight,
That oft beneath a light cloud sweeps along,
Lost for awhile, yet pours her varied song:
The eye still follows, and the cloud moves by,

Again he stretches up the clear blue sky;   100
His form, his motion, undistinguish'd quite,
Save when he wheels direct from shade to light:
E'en then the songster a mere speck became,
Gliding like fancy's bubbles in a dream,
The gazer sees; but yielding to repose,
Unwittingly his jaded eyelids close.
Delicious sleep! From sleep who could forbear,
With no more guilt than Giles, and no more care?
Peace o'er his slumbers waves her guardian wing,
Nor Conscience once disturbs him with a sting;   110
He wakes refresh'd from every trivial pain,
And takes his pole, and brushes round again.
    Its dark-green hue, its sicklier tints all fail,
And ripening Harvest rustles in the gale.
A glorious sight, if glory dwells below,
Where Heav'n's munificence makes all the show
O'er every field and golden prospect found,
That glads the Ploughman's Sunday morning's round,
When on some eminence he takes his stand,
To judge the smiling produce of the land.   120
Here Vanity slinks back, her head to hide;
What is there here to flatter human pride?
The tow'ring fabric, or the dome's loud roar,
And stedfast columns, may astonish more,
Where the charm'd gazer long delighted stays,
Yet trac'd but to the architect the praise;
Whilst here, the veriest clown that treads the sod,
Without one scruple gives the praise to God;
And twofold joys possess his raptur'd mind,
From gratitude and admiration join'd.   130
    Here, midst the boldest triumphs of her worth,
Nature herself invites the Reapers forth;
Dares the keen sickle from its twelvemonth's rest,
And gives that ardour which in every breast
From infancy to age alike appears,
When the first sheaf its plumy top uprears.
No rake takes here what Heaven to all bestows—
Children of want, for you the bounty flows!
And every cottage from the plenteous store

Receives a burden nightly at its door.   140
    Hark! where the sweeping scythe now rips along:
Each sturdy Mower, emulous and strong,
Whose writhing form meridian heat defies,
Bends o'er his work, and every sinew tries;
Prostrates the waving treasure at his feet,
But spares the rising clover, short and sweet.
Come Health! come, Jollity! light-footed, come;
Here hold your revels, and make this your home.
Each heart awaits and hails you as its own;
Each moisten'd brow, that scorns to wear a frown;   150
Th'unpeopled dwelling mourns its tenants stray'd;
E'en the domestic, laughing dairy-maid
Hies to the Field, the general toil to share.
Meanwhile the Farmer quits his elbow-chair,
His cool brick floor, his pitcher, and his ease,
And braves the sultry beams, and gladly sees
His gates thrown open, and his team abroad,
The ready group attendant on his word,
To turn the swarth, the quiv'ring load to rear,
Or ply the busy rake, the land to clear.   160
Summer's light garb itself now cumb'rous grown,
Each his thin doublet in the shade throws down;
Where oft the Mastiff sculks with half-shut eye,
And rouses at the stranger passing by;
Whilst unrestrain'd the social converse flows,
And every breast Love's powerful impulse knows,
And rival wits with more than rustic grace
Confess the presence of a pretty face.
    For, lo! encircled there, the lovely Maid,
In youth's own bloom and native smiles array'd;   170
Her hat awry, divested of her gown,
Her creaking stays of leather, stout and brown;—
Invidious barrier! Why art thou so high,
When the slight covering of her neck slips by,
There half revealing to the eager sight
Her full, ripe bosom, exquisitely white?
In many a local tale of harmless mirth,
And many a jest of momentary birth,
She bears a part, and as she stops to speak,

Strokes back the ringlets from her glowing cheek.   180
    Now noon gone by, and four declining hours,
The weary limbs relax their boasted pow'rs;
Thirst rages strong, the fainting spirits fail,
And ask the sov'reign cordial, home-brew'd ale:
Beneath some shelt'ring heap of yellow corn
Rests the hoop'd keg, and friendly cooling horn,
That mocks alike the goblet's brittle frame,
Its costlier potions, and its nobler name.
To Mary first the brimming draught is given,
By toil made welcome as the dews of heaven,   190
And never lip that press'd its homely edge
Had kinder blessings, or a heartier pledge.
    Of wholesome viands here a banquet smiles,
A common cheer for all;—e'en humble Giles,
Who joys his trivial services to yield
Amidst the fragrance of the open field;
Oft doom'd in suffocating heat to bear
The cobweb'd barn's impure and dusty air;
To ride in mirky state the panting steed,
Destin'd aloft th'unloaded grain to tread,   200
Where, in his path as heaps on heaps are thrown,
He rears, and plunges the loose mountain down:
Laborious task! with what delight, when done
Both horse and rider greet th'unclouded sun!
    Yet by th'unclouded sun are hourly bred
The bold assailants that surround thine head,
Poor, patient Ball! and with insulting wing
Roar in thine ears, and dart the piercing sting;
In thy behalf the crest-wav'd boughs avail
More than thy short-clipt remnant of a tail,   210
A moving mockery, a useless name,
A living proof of cruelty and shame.
Shame to the man, whatever fame he bore,
Who took from thee what man can ne'er restore,
Thy weapon of defence, thy chiefest good,
When swarming flies contending suck thy blood.
Nor thine alone the suff'ring, thine the care,
The fretful Ewe bemoans an equal share;
Tormented into sores, her head she hides,

Or angry sweeps them from her new-shorn sides.   220
Penn'd in the yard, e'en now at closing day
Unruly Cows with mark'd impatience stay,
And vainly striving to escape their foes,
The pail kick down; a piteous current flows.
    Is't not enough that plagues like these molest?
Must still another foe annoy their rest?
He comes, the pest and terror of the yard,
His full-fledg'd progeny's imperious guard;
The Gander;—spiteful, insolent, and bold,
At the colt's footlock takes his daring hold: 230
There, serpent like, escapes a dreadful blow;
And straight attacks a poor defenceless cow;
Each booby Goose th'unworthy strife enjoys,
And hails his prowess with redoubled noise.
Then back he stalks, of self-importance full,
Seizes the shaggy foretop of the Bull,
Till whirl'd aloft he falls: a timely check,
Enough to dislocate his worthless neck:
For lo! of old, he boasts an honour'd wound;
Behold that broken wing that trails the ground!   240
Thus fools and bravoes kindred pranks pursue;
As savage quite, and oft as fatal too.
Happy the man that foils an envious elf,
Using the darts of spleen to serve himself.
As when by turns the strolling Swine engage
The utmost efforts of the bully's rage,
Whose nibbling warfare on the grunter's side
Is welcome pleasure to his bristly hide;
Gently he stoops, or stretch'd at ease along,
Enjoys the insults of the gabbling throng,   250
That march exulting round his fallen head,
As human victors trample on their dead.
    Still Twilight, welcome! Rest, how sweet art thou!
Now eve o'erhangs the western cloud's thick brow:
The far-stretch'd curtain of retiring light,
With fiery treasures fraught; that on the sight
Flash from its bulging sides, where darkness lours,
In Fancy's eye, a chain of mould'ring tow'rs;
Or craggy coasts just rising into view,

Midst jav'lins dire, and darts of streaming blue.   260
    Anon tir'd laborers bless their shelt'ring home,
When Midnight, and the frightful Tempest come.
The Farmer wakes, and sees with silent dread
The angry shafts of Heaven gleam round his bed;
The bursting cloud reiterated roars,
Shakes his straw roof, and jars his bolted doors:
The slow-wing'd storm along the troubled skies
Spreads its dark course; the wind begins to rise;
And full-leaf'd elms, his dwelling's shade by day,
With mimic thunder give its fury way: 270
Sounds in his chimney-top a doleful peal
Midst pouring rain, or gusts of rattling hail;
With tenfold danger low the tempest bends
And quick and strong the sulph'rous flame descends:
The frighten'd Mastiff from his kennel flies,
And cringes at the door with piteous cries.—
    Where now's the trifler? where the child of pride?
These are the moments when the heart is try'd!
Nor lives the man, with conscience e'er so clear,
But feels a solemn, reverential fear;   280
Feels too a joy relieve his aching breast,
When the spent storm hath howl'd itself to rest.
Still, welcome beats the long-continued show'r,
And sleep protracted, comes with double pow'r;
Calm dreams of bliss bring on the morning sun,
For every barn is fill'd, and Harvest done!
    Now, ere sweet Summer bids its long adieu,
And winds blow keen where late the blossom grew,
The bustling day and jovial night must come,
The long-accustom'd feast of Harvest-home.   290
No blood-stain'd victory, in story bright,
Can give the philosophic mind delight;
No triumph please, while rage and death destroy:
Reflection sickens at the monstrous joy.
And where the joy, if rightly understood,
Like cheerful praise for universal good?
The soul nor check nor doubtful anguish knows,
But free and pure the grateful current flows.
    Behold the sound oak table's massy frame

Bestride the kitchen floor! the careful dame   300
And gen'rous host invite their friends around,
For all that clear'd the crop, or till'd the ground,
Are guests by right of custom:—old and young;
And many a neighbouring yeoman join the throng,
With artizans that lent their dext'rous aid,
When o'er each field the flaming sunbeams play'd.
    Yet Plenty reigns, and from her boundless hoard,
Though not one jelly trembles on the board,
Supplies the feast with all that sense can crave;
With all that made our great forefathers brave,   310
Ere the cloy'd palate countless flavours try'd,
And cooks had Nature's judgment set aside.
With thanks to Heaven, and tales of rustic lore,
The mansion echoes when the banquet's o'er;
A wider circle spreads, and smiles abound,
As quick the frothing horn performs its round;
Care's mortal foe; that sprightly joys imparts
To cheer the frame and elevate their hearts.
Here, fresh and brown, the hazel's produce lies
In tempting heaps, and peals of laughter rise,   320
And crackling Music, with the frequent Song,
Unheeded bear the midnight hour along.
    Here once a year Distinction low'rs its crest,
The master, servant, and the merry guest,
Are equal all; and round the happy ring
The reaper's eyes exulting glances fling,
And, warm'd with gratitude, he quits his place,
With sun-burnt hands and ale-enliven'd face,
Refills the jug his honour'd host to tend,
To serve at once the master and the friend;   330
Proud thus to meet his smiles, to share his tale,
His nuts, his conversation, and his ale.
    Such were the days,—of days long past I sing,
When Pride gave place to mirth without a sting;
Ere tyrant customs strength sufficient bore
To violate the feelings of the poor;
To leave them distanc'd in the mad'ning race,
Where'er refinement shows its hated face:
Nor causeless hated;—'tis the peasant's curse,

That hourly makes his wretched station worse;   340
Destroys life's intercourse; the social plan
That rank to rank cements, as man to man:
Wealth flows around him, Fashion lordly reigns;
Yet poverty is his, and mental pains.
  Methinks I hear the mourner thus impart
The stifled murmurs of his wounded heart:
'Whence comes this change, ungracious, irksome, cold?
Whence the new grandeur that mine eyes behold?
The widening distance which I daily see,
Has Wealth done this?—then Wealth's a foe to me;   350
Foe to our rights; that leaves a pow'rful few
The paths of emulation to pursue:—
For emulation stoops to us no more:
The hope of humble industry is o'er;
The blameless hope, the cheering sweet presage
Of future comforts for declining age.
Can my sons share from this paternal hand
The profits with the labours of the land?
No; though indulgent Heaven its blessing deigns,
Where's the small farm to suit my scanty means?   360
Content, the Poet sings, with us resides;
In lonely cots like mine, the Damsel hides;
And will he then in raptur'd visions tell
That sweet Content with Want can ever dwell?
A barley loaf, 'tis true, my table crowns,
That, fast diminishing in lusty rounds,
Stops Nature's cravings; yet her sighs will flow
From knowing this,—that once it was not so.
Our annual feast, when Earth her plenty yields,
When crown'd with boughs the last load quits the fields,   370
The aspect still of ancient joy puts on;
The aspect only, with the substance gone:
The self-same Horn is still at our command,
But serves none now but the plebeian hand:
For home-brew'd Ale, neglected and debas'd,
Is quite discarded from the realms of taste.
Where unaffected Freedom charm'd the soul,
The separate table and the costly bowl,
Cool as the blast that checks the budding Spring

A mockery of gladness round them fling.   380
For oft the Farmer, ere his heart approves,
Yields up the custom which he dearly loves:
Refinement forces on him like a tide;
Bold innovations down its current ride,
That bear no peace beneath their showy dress,
Nor add one tittle to his happiness.
His guests selected; rank's punctilios known;
What trouble waits upon a casual frown!
Restraint's foul manacles his pleasures maim;
Selected guests selected phrases claim: 390
Nor reigns that joy, when hand in hand they join,
That good old Master felt in shaking mine.
Heaven bless his memory! bless his honour'd name!
(The poor will speak his lasting worthy fame:)
To souls fair-purpos'd strength and guidance give;
In pity to us still let goodness live:
Let labour have its due! my cot shall be
From chilling want and guilty murmurs free:
Let labour have its due; then peace is mine,
And never, never shall my heart repine.'   400

AUTUMN. III

Argument. Acorns. Hogs in the Wood. Wheat-sowing. The Church. Village
Girls. The Mad Girl. The Bird-Boy's Hut. Disappointment; Reflections, &c.
Euston-hall. Fox-hunting. Old Trouncer. Long Nights. A Welcome to Winter.

Again, the year's decline, midst storms and floods,
The thundering chase, the yellow fading woods,
Invite my song; that fain would boldly tell
Of upland coverts, and the echoing dell,
By turns resounding loud, at eve and morn
The swineherd's halloo, or the huntsman's horn.
 No more the fields with scatter'd grain supply
The restless wandering tenants of the Sty;
From oak to oak they run with eager haste,
And wrangling share the first delicious taste   10
Of fallen Acorns; yet but thinly found
Till the strong gale has shook them to the ground.
It comes; and roaring woods obedient wave:
Their home well pleas'd the joint adventurers leave:
The trudging Sow leads forth her numerous young,
Playful, and white, and clean, the briars among,
Till briars and thorns increasing, fence them round,
Where last year's mould'ring leaves bestrew the ground,
And o'er their heads, loud lash'd by furious squalls,

Bright from their cups the rattling treasure falls;   20
Hot, thirsty food; whence double sweet and cool
The welcome margin of some rush-grown pool,
The Wild Duck's lonely haunt, whose jealous eye
Guards every point; who sits, prepar'd to fly,
On the calm bosom of her little lake,
Too closely screen'd for ruffian winds to shake;
And as the bold intruders press around,
At once she starts, and rises with a bound:
With bristles rais'd the sudden noise they hear,
And ludicrously wild, and wing'd with fear,   30
The herd decamp with more than swinish speed,
And snorting dash through sedge, and rush, and reed:
Through tangling thickets headlong on they go,
Then stop and listen for their fancied foe;
The hindmost still the growing panic spreads,
Repeated fright the first alarm succeeds,
Till Folly's wages, wounds and thorns, they reap:
Yet glorying in their fortunate escape,
Their groundless terrors by degrees soon cease,
And Night's dark reign restores their wonted peace.   40
For now the gale subsides, and from each bough
The roosting Pheasant's short but frequent crow
Invites to rest; and huddling side by side,
The herd in closest ambush seek to hide;
Seek some warm slope with shagged moss o'erspread,
Dry'd leaves their copious covering and their bed,
In vain may Giles, through gath'ring glooms that fall,
And solemn silence, urge his piercing call:
Whole days and nights they tarry midst their store,
Nor quit the woods till oaks can yield no more.   50
        Beyond bleak Winter's rage, beyond the Spring
That rolling Earth's unvarying course will bring,
Who tills the ground looks on with mental eye,
And sees next Summer's sheaves and cloudless sky;
And even now, whilst Nature's beauty dies,
Deposits Seed and bids new Harvests rise;
Seed well prepar'd, and warm'd with glowing lime,
'Gainst earth-bred grubs, and cold, and lapse of time:
For searching frosts and various ills invade,

Whilst wintry months depress the springing blade.   60
The plough moves heavily, and strong the soil,
And clogging harrows with augmented toil
Dive deep: and clinging, mixes with the mould
A fatt'ning treasure from the nightly fold,
And all the cow-yard's highly valu'd store,
That late bestrew'd the blacken'd surface o'er.
No idling hours are here, when Fancy trims
Her dancing taper over outstretch'd limbs,
And in her thousand thousand colours drest,
Plays round the grassy couch of noontide rest: 70
Here Giles for hours of indolence atones
With strong exertion, and with weary bones,
And knows no leisure; till the distant chime
Of Sabbath bells he hears at sermon time,
That down the brook sound sweetly in the gale,
Or strike the rising hill, or skim the dale.
    Nor his alone the sweets of ease to taste:
Kind rest extends to all;—save one poor beast,
That true to time and pace, is doom'd to plod,
To bring the Pastor to the House of God: 80
Mean structure; where no bones of heroes lie!
The rude inelegance of poverty
Reigns here alone: else why that roof of straw?
Those narrow windows with the frequent flaw?
O'er whose low cells the dock and mallow spread,
And rampant nettles lift the spiry head,
Whilst from the hollows of the tower on high
The gray-capp'd Daws in saucy legions fly.
    Round these lone walls assembling neighbours meet,
And tread departed friends beneath their feet;   90
And new-briar'd graves, that prompt the secret sigh,
Show each the spot where he himself must lie.
    Midst timely greetings village news goes round,
Of crops late shorn, or crops that deck the ground;
Experienc'd ploughmen in the circle join;
While sturdy boys, in feats of strength to shine,
With pride elate, their young associates brave
To jump from hollow-sounding grave to grave;
Then close consulting, each his talent lends

To plan fresh sports when tedious service ends.   100
   Hither at times, with cheerfulness of soul,
Sweet village Maids from neighbouring hamlets stroll,
That like the light-heel'd does o'er lawns that rove,
Look shyly curious; rip'ning into love;
For love's their errand: hence the tints that glow
On either cheek, a heighten'd lustre know:
When, conscious of their charms, e'en Age looks sly,
And rapture beams from Youth's observant eye.
   The Pride of such a party, Nature's pride,
Was lovely Ann; who innocently try'd,   110
With hat of airy shape and ribbons gay,
Love to inspire, and stand in Hymen's way:
But, ere her twentieth Summer could expand,
Or youth was render'd happy with her hand,
Her mind's serenity, her peace was gone,
Her eye grew languid, and she wept alone:
Yet causeless seem'd her grief; for quick restrain'd,
Mirth follow'd loud; or indignation reign'd:
Whims wild and simple led her from her home,
The heath, the common, or the fields to roam: 120
Terror and Joy alternate rul'd her hours;
Now blithe she sung, and gather'd useless flow'rs;
Now pluck'd a tender twig from every bough,
To whip the hov'ring demons from her brow.
Ill-fated Maid! thy guiding spark is fled,
And lasting wretchedness awaits thy bed—
Thy bed of straw! for mark, where even now
O'er their lost child afflicted parents bow;
Their woe she knows not, but perversely coy,
Inverted customs yield her sullen joy;   130
Her midnight meals in secrecy she takes,
Low mutt'ring to the moon, that rising breaks
Thro' night's dark gloom:—oh how much more forlorn
Her night, that knows of no returning morn!—
Slow from the threshold, once her infant seat,
O'er the cold earth she crawls to her retreat;
Quitting the cot's warm walls, unhous'd to lie,
Or share the swine's impure and narrow sty;
The damp night air her shiv'ring limbs assails;

In dreams she moans, and fancied wrongs bewails.   140
When morning wakes, none earlier rous'd than she,
When pendent drops fall glitt'ring from the tree;
But nought her rayless melancholy cheers,
Or sooths her breast, or stops her streaming tears.
Her matted locks unornamented flow;
Clasping her knees, and waving to and fro;—
Her head bow'd down, her faded cheek to hide;—
A piteous mourner by the pathway side.
Some tufted molehill through the livelong day
She calls her throne; there weeps her life away: 150
And oft the gaily-passing stranger stays
His well-tim'd step, and takes a silent gaze,
Till sympathetic drops unbidden start,
And pangs quick springing muster round his heart;
And soft he treads with other gazers round,
And fain would catch her sorrows' plaintive sound:
One word alone is all that strikes the ear,
One short, pathetic, simple word,—'Oh dear!'
A thousand times repeated to the wind,
That wafts the sigh, but leaves the pang behind!   160
For ever of the proffer'd parley shy,
She hears th'unwelcome foot advancing nigh;
Nor quite unconscious of her wretched plight,
Gives one sad look, and hurries out of sight.—
    Fair promis'd sunbeams of terrestrial bliss,
Health's gallant hopes,—and are ye sunk to this?
For in life's road though thorns abundant grow,
There still are joys poor Ann can never know;
Joys which the gay companions of her prime
Sip, as they drift along the stream of time;   170
At eve to hear beside their tranquil home
The lifted latch, that speaks the lover come:
That love matur'd, next playful on the knee
To press the velvet lips of infancy;
To stay the tottering step, the features trace;—
Inestimable sweets of social peace!
    O Thou, who bidst the vernal juices rise!
Thou, on whose blasts autumnal foliage flies!
Let Peace ne'er leave me, nor my heart grow cold,

Whilst life and sanity are mine to hold.   180
    Shorn of their flow'rs that shed th'untreasur'd seed,
The withering pasture, and the fading mead,
Less tempting grown, diminish more and more,
The dairy's pride; sweet Summer's flowing store.
New cares succeed, and gentle duties press,
Where the fire-side, a school of tenderness,
Revives the languid chirp, and warms the blood
Of cold-nipt weaklings of the latter brood,
That from the shell just bursting into day,
Through yard or pond pursue their vent'rous way.   190
    Far weightier cares and wider scenes expand;
What devastation marks the new-sown land!
'From hungry woodland foes go, Giles, and guard
The rising wheat: ensure its great reward:
A future sustenance, a Summer's pride,
Demand thy vigilance: then be it try'd:
Exert thy voice, and wield thy shotless gun:
Go, tarry there from morn till setting sun.'
    Keen blows the blast, or ceaseless rain descends;
The half-stript hedge a sorry shelter lends.   200
O for a Hovel, e'er so small or low,
Whose roof, repelling winds and early snow,
Might bring home's comforts fresh before his eyes!
No sooner thought, than see the structure rise,
In some sequester'd nook, embank'd around,
Sods for its walls, and straw in burdens bound:
Dried fuel hoarded is his richest store,
And circling smoke obscures his little door;
Whence creeping forth, to duty's call he yields,
And strolls the Crusoe of the lonely fields.   210
On whitethorns tow'ring, and the leafless rose,
A frost-nipt feast in bright vermilion glows:
Where clust'ring sloes in glossy order rise,
He crops the loaded branch; a cumbrous prize;
And o'er the flame the sputt'ring fruit he rests,
Placing green sods to seat the coming guests;
His guests by promise; playmates young and gay:—
But Ah! fresh pastimes lure their steps away!
He sweeps his hearth, and homeward looks in vain

Till feeling Disappointment's cruel pain,   220
His fairy revels are exchang'd for rage,
His banquet marr'd, grown dull his hermitage.
The field becomes his prison, till on high
Benighted birds to shades and coverts fly.
Midst air, health, daylight, can he prisoner be?
If fields are prisons, where is Liberty?
Here still she dwells, and here her votaries stroll;
But disappointed hope untunes the soul:
Restraints unfelt whilst hours of rapture flow,
When troubles press, to chains and barriers grow.   230
Look then from trivial up to greater woes;
From the poor bird-boy with his roasted sloes,
To where the dungeon'd mourner heaves the sigh;
Where not one cheering sun-beam meets his eye.
Though ineffectual pity thine may be,
No wealth, no pow'r, to set the captive free;
Though only to thy ravish'd sight is given
The radiant path that Howard trod to heaven;
Thy slights can make the wretched more forlorn,
And deeper drive affliction's barbed thorn.   240
Say not, 'I'll come and cheer thy gloomy cell
With news of dearest friends; how good, how well:
I'll be a joyful herald to thine heart:'
Then fail, and play the worthless trifler's part,
To sip flat pleasures from thy glass's brim,
And waste the precious hour that's due to him.
In mercy spare the base, unmanly blow:
Where can he turn, to whom complain of you?
Back to past joys in vain his thoughts may stray,
Trace and retrace the beaten, worn-out way,   250
The rankling injury will pierce his breast,
And curses on thee break his midnight rest.
    Bereft of song, and ever-cheering green,
The soft endearments of the Summer scene,
New harmony pervades the solemn wood,
Dear to the soul, and healthful to the blood:
For bold exertion follows on the sound
Of distant Sportsmen, and the chiding Hound;
First heard from kennel bursting, mad with joy,

Where smiling Euston boasts her good Fitzroy,   260
Lord of pure alms, and gifts that wide extend;
The farmer's patron, and the poor man's friend:
Whose Mansion glitters with the eastern ray,
Whose elevated temple points the way,
O'er slopes and lawns, the park's extensive pride,
To where the victims of the chase reside,
Ingulf'd in earth, in conscious safety warm,
Till lo! a plot portends their coming harm.
     In earliest hours of dark and hooded morn,
Ere yet one rosy cloud bespeaks the dawn,   270
Whilst far abroad the Fox pursues his prey,
He's doom'd to risk the perils of the day,
From his strong hold block'd out; perhaps to bleed,
Or owe his life to fortune or to speed.
For now the pack, impatient rushing on,
Range through the darkest coverts one by one;
Trace every spot; whilst down each noble glade
That guides the eye beneath a changeful shade,
The loit'ring sportsman feels th'instinctive flame,
And checks his steed to mark the springing game.   280
Midst intersecting cuts and winding ways
The huntsman cheers his dogs, and anxious strays
Where every narrow riding, even shorn,
Gives back the echo of his mellow horn:
Till fresh and lightsome, every power untried,
The starting fugitive leaps by his side,
His lifted finger to his ear he plies,
And the view-halloo bids a chorus rise
Of Dogs quick-mouth'd, and shouts that mingle loud
As bursting thunder rolls from cloud to cloud.   290
With ears erect, and chest of vig'rous mould,
O'er ditch, o'er fence, unconquerably bold,
The shining courser lengthens every bound,
And his strong foot-locks suck the moisten'd ground,
As from the confines of the wood they pour,
And joyous villages partake the roar.
O'er heath far stretch'd, or down, or valley low,
The stiff-limb'd peasant, glorying in the show,
Pursues in vain; where Youth itself soon tires,

Spite of the transports that the chase inspires: 300
For who unmounted long can charm the eye,
Or hear the music of the leading cry?
    Poor faithful Trouncer! thou canst lead no more;
All thy fatigues and all thy triumphs o'er!
Triumphs of worth, whose long-excelling fame
Was still to follow true the hunted game;
Beneath enormous oaks, Britannia's boast,
In thick, impenetrable coverts lost,
When the warm pack in fault'ring silence stood,
Thine was the note that rous'd the list'ning wood,   310
Rekindling every joy with tenfold force,
Through all the mazes of the tainted course.
Still foremost thou the dashing stream to cross,
And tempt along the animated horse;
Foremost o'er fen or level mead to pass,
And sweep the show'ring dew-drops from the grass;
Then bright emerging from the mist below
To climb the woodland hill's exulting brow.
    Pride of thy race! with worth far less than thine,
Full many human leaders daily shine!   320
Less faith, less constancy, less gen'rous zeal!—
Then no disgrace my humble verse shall feel,
Where not one lying line to riches bows,
Or poison'd sentiments from rancour flows;
Nor flowers are strewn around Ambition's car:
An honest Dog's a nobler theme by far.
Each sportsman heard the tidings with a sigh,
When Death's cold touch had stopt his tuneful cry;
And though high deeds, and fair exalted praise,
In memory liv'd, and flow'd in rustic lays,   330
Short was the strain of monumental woe:
'Foxes rejoice! here buried lies your foe!'
In safety hous'd throughout Night's length'ning reign,
The Cock sends forth a loud and piercing strain;
More frequent, as the glooms of midnight flee,
And hours roll round that brought him liberty,
When Summer's early dawn, mild, clear, and bright,
Chas'd quick away the transitory night:—
Hours now in darkness veil'd; yet loud the scream

Of Geese impatient for the playful stream;   340
And all the feather'd tribe imprison'd raise
Their morning notes of inharmonious praise;
And many a clamorous Hen and cockrel gay,
When daylight slowly through the fog breaks way,
Fly wantonly abroad: but, ah, how soon
The shades of twilight follow hazy noon,
Short'ning the busy day!—day that slides by
Amidst th'unfinish'd toils of Husbandry;
Toils still each morn resum'd with double care,
To meet the icy terrors of the year;   350
To meet the threats of Boreas undismay'd,
And Winter's gathering frowns and hoary head.
    Then welcome, Cold; welcome, ye snowy nights!
Heaven midst your rage shall mingle pure delights,
And confidence of hope the soul sustain,
While devastation sweeps along the plain:
Nor shall the child of poverty despair,
But bless The Power that rules the changing year,
Assur'd,—though horrors round his cottage reign,—
That Spring will come, and Nature smile again.   360

WINTER. IV

Argument. Tenderness to Cattle. Frozen Turnips. The Cow-yard. Night. The Farm-house. Fire-side. Farmer's Advice and Instruction. Nightly Cares of the Stable. Dobbin. The Post-horse. Sheep-stealing Dogs. Walks occasioned thereby. The Ghost. Lamb Time. Returning Spring. Conclusion.

With kindred pleasures mov'd, and cares opprest,
Sharing alike our weariness and rest;
Who lives the daily partner of our hours,
Through every change of heat, and frost, and show'rs;
Partakes our cheerful meals, partaking first
In mutual labour and fatigue and thirst;
The kindly intercourse will ever prove
A bond of amity and social love.
To more than man this generous warmth extends,
And oft the team and shiv'ring herd befriends;   10
Tender solicitude the bosom fills,
And Pity executes what Reason wills:
Youth learns compassion's tale from ev'ry tongue,
And flies to aid the helpless and the young.
  When now, unsparing as the scourge of war,
Blasts follow blasts, and groves dismantled roar,
Around their home the storm-pinch'd Cattle lows,
No nourishment in frozen pastures grows;
Yet frozen pastures every morn resound

With fair abundance thund'ring to the ground.   20
For though on hoary twigs no buds peep out,
And e'en the hardy brambles cease to sprout,
Beneath dread Winter's level sheets of snow
The sweet nutritious Turnip deigns to grow.
Till now imperious want and wide-spread dearth
Bid Labour claim her treasures from the earth.
On Giles, and such as Giles, the labour falls,
To strew the frequent load where hunger calls.
On driving gales sharp hail indignant flies,
And sleet, more irksome still, assails his eyes;   30
Snow clogs his feet; or if no snow is seen,
The field with all its juicy store to screen,
Deep goes the frost, till every root is found
A rolling mass of ice upon the ground.
No tender ewe can break her nightly fast,
Nor heifer strong begin the cold repast,
Till Giles with pond'rous beetle foremost go,
And scatt'ring splinters fly at every blow;
When pressing round him, eager for the prize,
From their mixt breath warm exhalations rise.   40
      In beaded rows if drops now deck the spray,
While the sun grants a momentary ray,
Let but a cloud's broad shadow intervene,
And stiffen'd into gems the drops are seen;
And down the furrow'd oak's broad southern side
Streams of dissolving rime no longer glide.
      Though Night approaching bids for rest prepare,
Still the flail echoes through the frosty air,
Nor stops till deepest shades of darkness come,
Sending at length the weary Labourer home.   50
From him, with bed and nightly food supplied,
Throughout the yard, hous'd round on every side,
Deep-plunging Cows their rustling feast enjoy,
And snatch sweet mouthfuls from the passing Boy,
Who moves unseen beneath his trailing load,
Fills the tall racks, and leaves a scatter'd road;
Where oft the swine from ambush warm and dry
Bolt out, and scamper headlong to their sty,
When Giles with well-known voice, already there,

Deigns them a portion of his evening care.   60
  Him, though the cold may pierce, and storms molest,
Succeeding hours shall cheer with warmth and rest;
Gladness to spread, and raise the grateful smile,
He hurls the faggot bursting from the pile,
And many a log and rifted trunk conveys,
To heap the fire, and wide extend the blaze,
That quivering strong through every opening flies,
Whilst smoky columns unobstructed rise.
For the rude architect, unknown to fame,
(Nor symmetry nor elegance his aim)   70
Who spreads his floors of solid oak on high,
On beams rough-hewn, from age to age that lie,
Bade his wide Fabric unimpair'd sustain
The orchard's store, and cheese, and golden grain;
Bade, from its central base, capacious laid,
The well-wrought chimney rear its lofty head;
Where since hath many a savoury ham been stor'd,
And tempests howl'd, and Christmas gambols roar'd.
  Flat on the hearth the glowing embers lie,
And flames reflected dance in every eye: 80
There the long billet, forc'd at last to bend,
While gushing sap froths out at either end,
Throws round its welcome heat:—the ploughman smiles,
And oft the joke runs hard on sheepish Giles,
Who sits joint tenant of the corner-stool,
The converse sharing, though in duty's school;
For now attentively 'tis his to hear
Interrogations from the Master's chair.
  'Left ye your bleating charge, when day-light fled,
Near where the hay-stack lifts its snowy head?   90
Whose fence of bushy furze, so close and warm,
May stop the slanting bullets of the storm.
For, hark! it blows; a dark and dismal night:
Heaven guide the trav'ller's fearful steps aright!
Now from the woods, mistrustful and sharp-ey'd,
The Fox in silent darkness seems to glide,
Stealing around us, list'ning as he goes,
If chance the Cock or stamm'ring Capon crows,
Or Goose, or nodding Duck, should darkling cry,

As if appriz'd of lurking danger nigh: 100
Destruction waits them, Giles, if e'er you fail
To bolt their doors against the driving gale.
Strew'd you (still mindful of th'unshelter'd head)
Burdens of straw, the cattle's welcome bed?
Thine heart should feel, what thou may'st hourly see,
That duty's basis is humanity.
Of pain's unsavoury cup though thou may'st taste,
(The wrath of Winter from the black north-east,)
Thine utmost suff'rings in the coldest day
A period terminates, and joys repay.   110
Perhaps e'en now, while here those joys we boast,
Full many a bark rides down the neighb'ring coast,
Where the high northern waves tremendous roar,
Drove down by blasts from Norway's icy shore.
The Sea-boy there, less fortunate than thou,
Feels all thy pains in all the gusts that blow;
His freezing hands now drench'd, now dry, by turns;
Now lost, now seen, the distant light that burns,
On some tall cliff uprais'd, a flaming guide,
That throws its friendly radiance o'er the tide.   120
His labours cease not with declining day,
But toils and perils mark his wat'ry way;
And whilst in peaceful dreams secure *we* lie,
The ruthless whirlwinds rage along the sky,
Round his head whistling;—and shalt thou repine,
While this protecting roof still shelters thine!'
       Mild, as the vernal show'r, his words prevail,
And aid the moral precept of his tale:
His wond'ring hearers learn, and ever keep
These first ideas of the restless deep: 130
And, as the opening mind a circuit tries,
Present felicities in value rise.
Increasing pleasures every hour they find,
The warmth more precious, and the shelter kind;
Warmth that long reigning bids the eyelids close,
As through the blood its balmy influence goes,
When the cheer'd heart forgets fatigues and cares,
And drowsiness alone dominion bears.
       Sweet then the ploughman's slumbers, hale and young,

When the last topic dies upon his tongue;   140
Sweet then the bliss his transient dreams inspire,
Till chilblains wake him, or the snapping fire:
    He starts, and ever thoughtful of his team,
Along the glitt'ring snow a feeble gleam
Shoots from his lantern, as he yawning goes
To add fresh comforts to their night's repose;
Diffusing fragrance as their food he moves,
And pats the jolly sides of those he loves.
Thus full replenish'd, perfect ease possest,
From night till morn alternate food and rest,   150
No rightful cheer withheld, no sleep debarr'd,
Their each day's labour brings its sure reward.
Yet when from plough or lumb'ring cart set free,
They taste awhile the sweets of liberty:
E'en sober Dobbin lifts his clumsy heel
And kicks, disdainful of the dirty wheel;
But soon, his frolic ended, yields again
To trudge the road, and wear the clinking chain.
    Short-sighted Dobbin!—thou canst only see
The trivial hardships that encompass thee: 160
Thy chains were freedom, and thy toils repose:
Could the poor post-horse tell thee all his woes;
Show thee his bleeding shoulders, and unfold
The dreadful anguish he endures for gold:
Hir'd at each call of business, lust, or rage,
That prompts the trav'ller on from stage to stage.
Still on *his* strength depends their boasted speed;
For them his limbs grow weak, his bare ribs bleed;
And though he groaning quickens at command,
Their extra shilling in the rider's hand   170
Becomes his bitter scourge,—'tis *he* must feel
The double efforts of the lash and steel;
Till when, up hill, the destin'd inn he gains,
And trembling under complicated pains,
Prone from his nostrils, darting on the ground,
His breath emitted floats in clouds around:
Drops chase each other down his chest and sides,
And spatter'd mud his native colour hides:
Through his swoln veins the boiling torrent flows,

And every nerve a separate torture knows.   180
His harness loos'd, he welcomes, eager-eyed,
The pail's full draught that quivers by his side;
And joys to see the well-known stable door,
As the starv'd mariner the friendly shore.
    Ah, well for him if here his suff'rings ceas'd,
And ample hours of rest his pains appeas'd!
But rous'd again, and sternly bade to rise,
And shake refreshing slumber from his eyes,
Ere his exhausted spirits can return,
Or through his frame reviving ardour burn,   190
Come forth he must, though limping, maim'd, and sore;
He hears the whip; the chaise is at the door:—
The collar tightens, and again he feels
His half-heal'd wounds inflam'd; again the wheels
With tiresome sameness in his ears resound,
O'er blinding dust, or miles of flinty ground.
Thus nightly robb'd, and injur'd day by day,
His piece-meal murderers wear his life away.
What say'st thou Dobbin? what though hounds await
With open jaws the moment of thy fate,   200
No better fate attends *his* public race;
His life is misery, and his end disgrace.
Then freely bear thy burden to the mill;
Obey but one short law,—thy driver's will.
Affection to thy memory ever true,
Shall boast of mighty loads that Dobbin drew;
And back to childhood shall the mind with pride
Recount thy gentleness in many a ride
To pond, or field, or Village-fair, when thou
Held'st high thy braided mane and comely brow;   210
And oft the Tale shall rise to homely fame
Upon thy gen'rous spirit and thy name.
    Though faithful to a proverb, we regard
The midnight Chieftain of the farmer's yard,
Beneath whose guardianship all hearts rejoice,
Woke by the echo of his hollow voice;
Yet as the Hound may fault'ring quit the pack,
Snuff the foul scent, and hasten yelping back;
And e'en the docile Pointer know disgrace,

Thwarting the gen'ral instinct of his race;   220
E'en so the Mastiff, or the meaner Cur,
At time will from the path of duty err,
(A pattern of fidelity by day,
By night a murderer, lurking for his prey;)
And round the pastures or the fold will creep,
And, coward-like, attack the peaceful sheep.
Alone the wanton mischief he pursues,
Alone in reeking blood his jaws imbrues;
Chasing amain his frighten'd victims round,
Till death in wild confusion strews the ground;   230
Then wearied out, to kennel sneaks away,
And licks his guilty paws till break of day.
    The deed discover'd, and the news once spread,
Vengeance hangs o'er the unknown culprit's head:
And careful Shepherds extra hours bestow
In patient watchings for the common foe;
A foe most dreaded now, when rest and peace
Should wait the season of the flock's increase.
    In part these nightly terrors to dispel,
Giles, ere he sleeps, his little flock must tell.   240
From the fire-side with many a shrug he hies,
Glad if the full-orb'd Moon salute his eyes,
And through th'unbroken stillness of the night
Shed on his path her beams of cheering light.
With saunt'ring step he climbs the distant stile,
Whilst all around him wears a placid smile;
There views the white-rob'd clouds in clusters driven,
And all the glorious pageantry of Heaven.
Low, on the utmost bound'ry of the sight,
The rising vapours catch the silver light;   250
Thence Fancy measures, as they parting fly,
Which first will throw its shadow on the eye,
Passing the source of light; and thence away,
Succeeded quick by brighter still than they.
Far yet above these wafted clouds are seen
(In a remoter sky, still more serene,)
Others, detach'd in ranges through the air,
Spotless as snow, and countless as they're fair;
Scatter'd immensely wide from east to west,

The beauteous 'semblance of a Flock at rest.   260
These, to the raptur'd mind, aloud proclaim
Their Mighty Shepherd's everlasting Name.
    Whilst thus the loit'rer's utmost stretch of soul
Climbs the still clouds, or passes those that roll,
And loos'd Imagination soaring goes
High o'er his home, and all his little woes,
Time glides away; neglected Duty calls;
At once from plains of light to earth he falls,
And down a narrow lane, well known by day,
With all his speed pursues his sounding way,   270
In thought still half absorb'd, and chill'd with cold;
When lo! an object frightful to behold;
A grisly Spectre, cloth'd in silver-grey,
Around whose feet the waving shadows play,
Stands in his path!—He stops, and not a breath
Heaves from his heart, that sinks almost to death.
Loud the Owl halloos o'er his head unseen;
All else is silent, dismally serene:
Some prompt ejaculation, whisper'd low,
Yet bears him up against the threat'ning foe;   280
And thus poor Giles, though half inclin'd to fly,
Mutters his doubts, and strains his stedfast eye.
'Tis not my crimes thou com'st here to reprove;
No murders stain my soul, no perjur'd love:
If thou'rt indeed what here thou seem'st to be,
Thy dreadful mission cannot reach to me.
By parents taught still to mistrust mine eyes,
Still to approach each object of surprise,
Lest Fancy's formful visions should deceive
In moon-light paths, or glooms of falling eve,   290
This then's the moment when my mind should try
To scan thy motionless deformity;
But oh, the fearful task! yet well I know
An aged Ash, with many a spreading bough,
(Beneath whose leaves I've found a Summer's bow'r,
Beneath whose trunk I've weather'd many a show'r,)
Stands singly down this solitary way,
But far beyond where now my footsteps stay.
'Tis true, thus far I've come with heedless haste;

No reck'ning kept, no passing objects trac'd:—   300
And can I then have reach'd that very tree?
Or is its reverend form assum'd by thee?'
The happy thought alleviates his pain:
He creeps another step; then stops again;
Till slowly, as his noiseless feet draw near,
Its perfect lineaments at once appear;
Its crown of shiv'ring ivy whispering peace,
And its white bark that fronts the moon's pale face.
Now, whilst his blood mounts upward, now he knows
The solid gain from that conviction flows;   310
And strengthen'd Confidence shall hence fulfil
(With conscious Innocence more valued still)
The dreariest task that winter nights can bring,
By church-yard dark, or grove, or fairy ring;
Still buoying up the timid mind of youth,
Till loit'ring Reason hoists the scale of Truth.
With these blest guardians Giles his course pursues,
Till numbering his heavy-sided ewes,
Surrounding stillness tranquillize his breast,
And shape the dreams that wait his hours of rest.   320
        As when retreating tempests we behold,
Whose skirts at length the azure sky unfold,
And full of murmurings and mingled wrath,
Slowly unshroud the smiling face of earth,
Bringing the bosom joy: so Winter flies!—
And see, the Source of Life and Light uprise!
A height'ning arch o'er southern hills he bends;
Warm on the cheek the slanting beam descends,
And gives the reeking mead a brighter hue,
And draws the modest primrose bud to view.   330
Yet frosts succeed, and winds impetuous rush,
And hail-storms rattle through the budding bush;
And night-fall'n Lambs require the shepherd's care,
And teeming Ewes, that still their burdens bear;
Beneath whose sides to-morrow's dawn may see
The milk-white strangers bow the trembling knee;
At whose first birth the pow'rful instinct's seen
That fills with champions the daisied green:
For Ewes that stood aloof with fearful eye,

With stamping foot now Men and Dogs defy,   340
And obstinately faithful to their young,
Guard their first steps to join the bleating throng.
     But casualties and death from damps and cold
Will still attend the well-conducted fold:
Her tender offspring dead, the Dam aloud
Calls, and runs wild amidst th'unconscious crowd:
And orphan'd sucklings raise the piteous cry;
No wool to warm them, no defenders nigh.
And must her streaming milk then flow in vain?
Must unregarded innocence complain?   350
No;—ere this strong solicitude subside,
Maternal fondness may be fresh apply'd,
And the adopted stripling still may find
A parent most assiduously kind.
For this he's doom'd awhile disguis'd to range,
(For fraud or force must work the wish'd-for change;)
For this his predecessor's skin he wears,
Till, cheated into tenderness and cares,
The unsuspecting dam, contented grown,
Cherish and guard the fondling as her own.   360
     Thus all by turns to fair perfection rise;
Thus twins are parted to increase their size:
Thus instinct yields as interest points the way,
Till the bright flock, augmenting every day;
On sunny hills and vales of springing flow'rs
With ceaseless clamour greet the vernal hours.
     The humbler Shepherd here with joy beholds
Th'approv'd economy of crowded folds,
And, in his small contracted round of cares,
Adjusts the practice of each hint he hears: 370
For Boys with emulation learn to glow,
And boast their pastures, and their healthful show
Of well-grown Lambs, the glory of the Spring;
And field to field in competition bring.
     E'en Giles, for all his cares and watchings past,
And all his contests with the wintry blast,
Claims a full share of that sweet praise bestow'd
By gazing neighbours, when along the road,
Or village green, his curly-coated throng

Suspends the chorus of the Spinner's song;   380
When Admiration's unaffected grace
Lisps from the tongue, and beams in ev'ry face:
Delightful moments!—Sunshine, Health and Joy,
Play round, and cheer the elevated Boy!
'Another Spring!' his heart exulting cries;
'Another Year!' with promis'd blessings rise!—
'Eternal Power! from whom those blessings flow,
Teach me still more to wonder, more to know:
Seed-time and Harvest let me see again;
Wander the leaf-strewn wood, the frozen plain: 390
Let the first flower, corn-waving field, plain, tree,
Here round my home, still lift my soul to Thee;
And let me ever, midst thy bounties, raise
An humble note of thankfulness and praise!'—
                April 22, 1798.

From *Rural Tales* (1802)

From the Preface (1802)

The Poems here offered to the public were chiefly written during the interval between the concluding, and the publishing of 'the Farmer's Boy,' an interval of nearly two years. The pieces of a later date are, 'the Widow to her Hour-Glass,' 'The Fakenham Ghost,' 'Walter and Jane,' &c. At the time of publishing the Farmer's Boy, circumstances occurred which rendered it necessary to submit these poems to the perusal of my Friends: under whose approbation I now give them, with some confidence as to their moral merit, to the judgment of the public. And as they treat of village manners, and rural scenes, it appears to me not ill-tim'd to avow, that I have hopes of meeting in some degree the approbation of my Country. I was not prepar'd for the decided, and I may surely say extraordinary attention which The Public has shewn towards the Farmer's Boy: the consequence has been such as my true friends will rejoice to hear; it has produc'd me many essential blessings. And I feel peculiarly gratified in finding that a poor man in England may assert the dignity of Virtue, and speak of the imperishable beauties of Nature, and be heard, and heard, perhaps, with greater attention for his being poor...

I have received many honourable testimonies of esteem from strangers; letters without a name, but fill'd with the most cordial advice, and almost a parental anxiety, for my safety under so great a share of public applause. I beg to refer such friends to the great teacher Time: and hope that he will hereafter give me my deserts, and no more...

Preface to Poems (1809), Volume II

What now forms the first part of this Volume, was published in 1802 under the title of 'Rural Tales,' and the remainder in 1806 under the name of 'Wild Flowers'. Several pieces in the first collection, which the Public have sanctioned by a long and generous approbation, were written before the publication of the 'Farmer's Boy;' and consequently before I had friends to thank, or failures to dread. The original MSS. of these Poems are now in my possession, and I find therein, that seven years ago, I made memorandums which are now useful. Two or three of these detached sentences, as they are unvarnished truths, may afford amusement:—

'Remember having a great conceit of the "Miller's Maid;"—but of "Richard and Kate" I expected to hear a different account; was afraid it might be *too low*, as the critics call it, though for the life of me I can't tell what they mean by it. - - - - - - Began to think of the pleasure of an old couple meeting their grown-up children, and accordingly composed, or rather they composed themselves, the stanzas containing Richard's speech to his Sons and Daughters, which always pleased me best of any in the Ballad; I then began the opening of the Ballad, and filled up the chinks; for I had arranged two or three stanzas descriptive of their journey, particularly the ninth and tenth.

When I began the "Miller's Maid" I had no thought of making so long, or so good, a story of it. Had not thought of any plot or developement, but first of all wrote the girl's story, to try how far I could make a child's language touch my own feelings. The execrable usage of some Workhouse-Children, as stated in the newspapers, gave the thought at first. This plan was enlarged till it became the favourite of my heart, and cost me more tears than all the rest.

"The Widow," though it stands next in the printed copies, was not written next; it has nothing remarkable belonging to it, but that it is the only piece in the book which was written quick. Had an Hour-glass before me; my wife singing softly; my girls at school. Made a shoe between dinner and tea-time, and composed the "Widow" beside.'

The Reader will perceive, from these specimens, the design and tenor of my entries; they were private: and he is not troubled with them entirely without cause. Inquiries, such as these memorandums are calculated to satisfy, have often been made; and as the parties are as welcome to the Anecdotes as to the Poems, I find this the most ready and general way of compliance. It will also be recollected, that I am not here writing for the purpose of introducing the Poems to notice; they are already known, and must *stand or fall by themselves*, in spite of this or any other kind of Preface.   Robert Bloomfield. City Road, March, 1809.

RICHARD AND KATE; OR, FAIR-DAY. A SUFFOLK BALLAD

I

'Come, Goody, stop your humdrum wheel,
Sweep up your orts, and get your hat;
Old joys reviv'd once more I feel,
'Tis Fair-day;—ay, *and more than that.*

II

Have you forgot, Kate, prithee say,
How many Seasons here we've tarried?
'Tis *Forty* years, this very day,
Since you and I, old Girl, were married!

III

Look out; the Sun shines warm and bright,
The Stiles are low, the Paths all dry;
I know you cut your corns last night:
Come; be as free from care as I.

10

IV

For I'm resolv'd once more to see
That place where we so often met;
Though few have had more cares than we,
We've none just now to make us fret.'

V

Kate scorn'd to damp the generous flame
That warm'd her aged Partner's breast:
Yet, ere determination came,
She thus some trifling doubts express'd: 20

VI

'Night will come on; when seated snug,
And you've perhaps begun some tale,
Can you then leave your dear stone mug;
Leave all the folks, and all the ale?'

VII

'Ay, Kate, I wool;—because I know,
Though time has been we both could run,   ·
Such days are gone and over now;—
I only mean to see the fun.'

VIII

She straight slipp'd off the Wall and Band,
And laid aside her Lucks and Twitches: 30
And to the Hutch she reach'd her hand,
And gave him out his Sunday Breeches.

IX

His Mattock he behind the door
And Hedging-gloves again replac'd;
And look'd across the yellow Moor,
And urg'd his tott'ring Spouse to haste.

X

The day was up, the air serene,
The Firmament without a cloud;
The Bee humm'd o'er the level green,
Where knots of trembling Cowslips bow'd.   40

XI

And Richard thus, with heart elate,
As past things rush'd across his mind,
Over his shoulder talk'd to Kate,
Who, snug tuckt up, walk'd slow behind.

XII

'When once a giggling Mawther you,
And I a red-fac'd chubby Boy,
Sly tricks you play'd me not a few;
For mischief was your greatest joy.

XIII

Once, passng by this very Tree,
A Gotch of Milk I'd been to fill,   50
You shoulder'd me; then laugh'd to see
Me and my Gotch spin down the Hill.'

XIV

''Tis true,' she said; 'But here behold,
And marvel at the course of Time;
Though you and I are both grown old,
This Tree is only in its prime!'

XV

'Well, Goody, don't stand preaching now;
Folks don't preach Sermons at a Fair:
We've rear'd Ten Boys and Girls you know;
And I'll be bound they'll all be there.'   60

XVI

Now friendly nods and smiles had they,
From many a kind Fair-going face:
And many a pinch Kate gave away,
While Richard kept his usual pace.

XVII

At length arriv'd amidst the throng,
Grand-children bawling hemm'd them round;
And dragg'd them by the skirts along
Where gingerbread bestrew'd the ground.

XVIII

And soon the aged couple spy'd
Their lusty Sons, and Daughters dear: —   70
When Richard thus exulting cried,
'Did'nt I tell you they'd be here?'

XIX

The cordial greetings of the soul
Were visible in every face:
Affection, void of all controul,
Govern'd with a resistless grace.

XX

'Twas good to see the honest strife,
Which should contribute most to please;
And hear the long-recounted life,
Of infant tricks, and happy days.   80

XXI

But now, as at some nobler places,
Amongst the Leaders 'twas decreed
Time to begin the Dicky Races;
More fam'd for laughter than for speed.

XXII

Richard look'd on with wond'rous glee,
And prais'd the Lad who chanc'd to win;
'Kate, wa'n't I such a one as he?
As like him, ay, as pin to pin.

XXIII

Full Fifty years are pass'd away
Since I rode this same ground about;   90
Lord! I was lively as the day!
'I won the High-lows out and out!

XXIV

I'm surely growing young again:
I feel myself so kedge and plump.
From head to foot I've not one pain;
Nay, hang me if I cou'dn't jump.'

XXV

Thus spoke the Ale in Richard's pate,
A very little made him mellow;
But still he lov'd his faithful Kate,
Who whisper'd thus, 'My good old fellow,   100

XXVI

Remember what you promis'd me
And see, the Sun is getting low;
The Children want an hour ye see
To talk a bit before we go.'

XXVII

Like youthful Lover most complying
He turn'd, and chuckt her by the chin:
Then all across the green grass hying,
Right merry faces, all akin.

XXVIII

Their farewell quart, beneath a tree
That droop'd its branches from above,   110
Awak'd the pure felicity
That waits upon Parental Love.

XXIX

Kate view'd her blooming Daughters round,
And Sons, who shook her wither'd hand:
Her features spoke what joy she found;
But utterance had made a stand.

XXX

The Children toppled on the green,
And bowl'd their fairings down the hill;
Richard with pride beheld the scene,
Nor could he for his life sit still.   120

XXXI

A Father's uncheck'd feelings gave
A tenderness to all he said;
'My Boys, how proud am I to have
My name thus round the country spread!

XXXII

Through all my days I've labour'd hard,
And could of pains and crosses tell;
But this is Labour's great reward,
To meet ye thus, and see ye well.

XXXIII

My good old Partner, when at home,
Sometimes with wishes mingles tears;   130
Goody, says I, let what wool come,
We've nothing for them but our pray'rs.

XXXIV

May you be all as old as I,
And see your Sons to manhood grow;
And, many a time before you die,
Be just as pleas'd as I am now.'

XXXV

Then, (raising still his Mug and Voice,)
'An Old Man's weakness don't despise!
I love you well, my Girls and Boys;
God bless you all;'—so said his eyes—   140

XXVI

For as he spoke, a big round drop
Fell, bounding on his ample sleeve;
A witness which he could not stop,
A witness which all hearts believe.

XXVII

Thou, Filial Piety, wert there;
And round the ring, benignly bright,
Dwelt in the luscious half-shed tear,
And in the parting word—Good Night!

XXVIII

With thankful Hearts and strengthen'd Love,
The poor old Pair, supremely blest,   150
Saw the Sun sink behind the grove,
And gain'd once more their lowly rest.

THE WIDOW TO HER HOUR-GLASS

I

Come, friend, I'll turn thee up again:
Companion of the lonely hour!
Spring thirty times hath fed with rain
And cloth'd with leaves my humble bower,
    Since thou hast stood
    In frame of wood,
On Chest or Window by my side:
At every Birth still thou wert near,
Still spoke thine admonitions clear—
    And, when my Husband died,   10

II

I've often watch'd thy streaming sand
And seen the growing Mountain rise,
And often found Life's hopes to stand
On props as weak in Wisdom's eyes:
       Its conic crown
       Still sliding down,
Again heap'd up, then down again;
The sand above more hollow grew,
Like days and years still filt'ring through,
       And mingling joy and pain.   20

III

While thus I spin and sometimes sing
(For now and then my heart will glow)
Thou measur'st Time's expanding wing:
By thee the noontide hour I know:
       Though silent thou,
       Still shalt thou flow,
And jog along thy destin'd way:
But when I glean the sultry fields,
When Earth her yellow Harvest yields,
       Thou get'st a Holiday.   30

IV

Steady as Truth, on either end
Thy daily task performing well,
Thou'rt Meditation's constant friend,
And strik'st the Heart without a Bell:
       Come, lovely May!
       Thy lengthen'd day
Shall gild once more my native plain;
Curl inward here, sweet Woodbine flower;—
Companion of the lonely hour,
       I'll turn thee up again.   40

THE FAKENHAM GHOST. A BALLAD

This Ballad is founded on a fact. The circumstance occurred perhaps long before I was born; but is still related by my Mother, and some of the oldest inhabitants in that part of the country. R.B.

I

The Lawns were dry in Euston Park;
(Here Truth inspires my Tale)
The lonely footpath, still and dark,
Led over Hill and Dale.

II

Benighted was an ancient Dame,
And fearful haste she made
To gain the vale of Fakenham,
And hail its Willow shade.

III

Her footsteps knew no idle stops,
But follow'd faster still;   10
And echo'd to the darksome Copse
That whisper'd on the Hill;

IV

Where clam'rous Rooks, yet scarcely hush'd,
Bespoke a peopled shade;
And many a wing the foliage brush'd,
And hov'ring circuits made.

V

The dappled herd of grazing Deer
That sought the Shades by day,
Now started from her path with fear,
And gave the Stranger way.   20

VI

Darker it grew; and darker fears
Came o'er her troubled mind;
When now, a short quick step she hears
Come patting close behind.

VII

She turn'd; it stopt!—nought could she see
Upon the gloomy plain!
But, as she strove the Sprite to flee,
She heard the same again.

VIII

Now terror seiz'd her quaking frame:
For, where the path was bare,   30
The trotting Ghost kept on the same!
She mutter'd many a pray'r.

IX

Yet once again, amidst her fright
She tried what sight could do;
When through the cheating glooms of night,
A Monster stood in view.

X

Regardless of whate'er she felt,
It follow'd down the plain!
She own'd her sins, and down she knelt,
And said her pray'rs again.   40

XI

Then on she sped: and Hope grew strong,
The white park-gate in view;
Which pushing hard, so long it swung
That Ghost and all pass'd through.

XII

Loud fell the gate against the post!
Her heart-strings like to crack:
For, much she fear'd the grisly Ghost
Would leap upon her back.

XIII

Still on, pat, pat, the Goblin went,
As it had done before:—   50
Her strength and resolution spent,
She fainted at the door.

XIV

Out came her Husband, much surpris'd:
Out came her Daughter dear:
Good-natur'd Souls! all unadvis'd
Of what they had to fear.

XV

The Candle's gleam pierc'd through the night,
Some short space o'er the green;
And there the little trotting Sprite
Distinctly might be seen.   60

XVI

An *Ass's Foal* had lost its Dam
Within the spacious Park;
And simple as the playful Lamb,
Had follow'd in the dark.

XVII

No Goblin he; no imp of sin:
No crimes had ever known.
They took the shaggy stranger in,
And rear'd him as their own.

XVIII

His little hoofs would rattle round
Upon the Cottage floor: 70
The Matron learn'd to love the sound
That frighten'd her before.

XIX

A favorite the Ghost became;
And, 'twas his fate to thrive:
And long he liv'd and spread his fame,
And kept the joke alive.

XX

For many a laugh went through the Vale;
And some conviction too:—
Each thought some other Goblin tale,
Perhaps, was just as true.   80

WINTER SONG

I

Dear Boy, throw that Icicle down,
    And sweep this deep snow from the door:
Old Winter comes on with a frown;
    A terrible frown for the poor.
In a Season so rude and forlorn,
    How can age, how can infancy bear
The silent neglect and the scorn
    Of those who have plenty to spare?

II

Fresh broach'd is my Cask of old Ale,
    Well-tim'd now the frost is set in;   10
Here's Job come to tell us a tale,
    We'll make him at home to a pin.
While my Wife and I bask o'er the fire,
    The roll of the Seasons will prove,
That Time may diminish desire,
    But cannot extinguish true love.

III

O the pleasures of neighbourly chat,
    If you can but keep scandal away,
To learn what the world has been at,
    And what the great Orators say;   20
Though the Wind through the crevices sing,
    And Hail down the chimney rebound;
I'm happier than many a king
    While the Bellows blow Bass to the sound.

IV

Abundance was never my lot:
    But out of the trifle that's given,
That no curse may alight on my Cot,
    I'll distribute the bounty of Heav'n;
The fool and the slave gather wealth:
    But if I add nought to my store,   30
Yet while I keep conscience in health,
    I've a Mine that will never grow poor.

From *Good Tidings; or, News from the Farm* (1804)

Advertisement

To the few who know that I have employed my thoughts on the importance of Dr. Jenner's discovery, it has generally and almost unexceptionably appeared a subject of little promise; peculiarly unfit indeed for poetry. My method of treating it has endeared it to myself, for it indulges in domestic anecdote. The account given of my infancy, and of my father's burial, is not only poetically, but strictly true, and with me it has its weight accordingly. I have witnessed the destruction described in my brother's family; and I have, in my own, insured the lives of four children by Vaccine Inoculation, who, I trust, are destined to look back upon the Small-pox as the scourge of days gone by.—My hopes are high, and my prayers sincere, for its universal adoption.

The few notes subjoined are chiefly from 'Woodville on Inoculation;' and if I may escape the appearance of affectation of research, or a scientific treatment of the subject, I think the egotism, so conspicuous in the poem, (as facts give force to argument,) ought to be forgiven.

[i. The child who has been blinded by smallpox]

Where's the Blind Child, so admirably fair,
With guileless dimples, and with flaxen hair
That waves in ev'ry breeze? he's often seen
Beside yon cottage wall, or on the green,
With others match'd in spirit and in size,
Health on their cheeks, and rapture in their eyes;
That full expanse of voice, to childhood dear,
Soul of their sports, is duly cherish'd here:
And, hark! that laugh is his, that jovial cry;
He hears the ball and trundling hoop brush by,   10
And runs the giddy course with all his might,
A very child in every thing but sight;
With circumscrib'd, but not abated pow'rs,—
Play! the great object of his infant hours;—
In many a game he takes a noisy part,

And shows the native gladness of his heart;
But soon he hears, on pleasure all intent,
The new suggestion and the quick assent;
The grove invites, delight thrills every breast—
To leap the ditch and seek the downy nest   20
Away they start, leave balls and hoops behind,
And one companion leave—the boy is blind!
His fancy paints their distant paths so gay,
That childish fortitude awhile gives way,
He feels his dreadful loss—yet short the pain,
Soon he resumes his cheerfulness again;
Pond'ring how best his moments to employ,
He sings his little songs of nameless joy,
Creeps on the warm green turf for many an hour,
And plucks by chance the white and yellow flow'r;   30
Smoothing their stems, while resting on his knees,
He binds a nosegay which he never sees;
Along the homeward path then feels his way,
Lifting his brow against the shining day,
And, with a playful rapture round his eyes,
Presents a sighing parent with the prize.
      She blest *that* day, which he remembers too,
When he could gaze on heav'n's ethereal blue,
See the green Spring, and Summer's countless dies,
And all the colours of the morning rise.—   40
'When was this work of bitterness begun?
How came the blindness of your only son?'
Thus pity prompts full many a tongue to say,
But never, till she slowly wipes away
Th'obtruding tear that trembles in her eye,
This dagger of a question meets reply:—
'My boy was healthy, and my rest was sound,
When last year's corn was green upon the ground:
From yonder town infection found its way;
Around me putrid dead and dying lay.   50
I trembled for his fate: but all my care
Avail'd not, for he breath'd the tainted air;
Sickness ensu'd—in terror and dismay
I nurs'd him in my arms both night and day,
When his soft skin from head to foot became

One swelling purple sore, unfit to name:
Hour after hour, when all was still beside,
When the pale night-light in its socket died,
Alone I sat; the thought still sooths my heart,
That surely I perform'd a mother's part,   60
Watching with such anxiety and pain
Till he might smile and look on me again;
But that was not to be—ask me no more:
God keep small-pox and blindness from your door!'

[ii. The discovery of inoculation and vaccination]

Dear must that moment be when first the mind,
Ranging the paths of science unconfin'd,
Strikes a new light; when, obvious to the sense,
Springs the fresh spark of bright intelligence.
So felt the towering soul of Montagu,
Her sex's glory, and her country's too;
Who gave the spotted plague one deadly blow,
And bade its mitigated poison flow
With half its terrors; yet, with loathing still,
We hous'd a visitant with pow'r to kill.   10
Then when the healthful blood, though often tried,
Foil'd the keen lancet by the Severn side,
Resisting, uncontaminated still,
The purple pest and unremitting skill;
When the plain truth tradition seem'd to know,
By simply pointing to the harmless Cow,
Though wise distrust to reason might appeal;
What, when hope triumph'd, what did Jenner feel!
Where even hope itself could scarcely rise
To scan the vast, inestimable prize!   20

[iii. Smallpox is brought into the poet's home, and strikes down his father]

There dwelt, beside a brook that creeps along
Midst infant hills and meads unknown to song,
One to whom poverty and faith were giv'n,
Calm village silence, and the hope of heav'n:
Alone she dwelt; and while each morn brought peace,

And health was smiling on her year's increase,
Sudden and fearful, rushing through her frame,
Unusual pains and feverish symptoms came.
Then, when debilitated, faint, and poor,
How sweet to hear a footstep at her door!   10
To see a neighbour watch life's silent sand,
To hear the sigh, and feel the helping hand!
Soon woe o'erspread the interdicted ground,
And consternation seiz'd the hamlets round:
Uprose the pest—its widow'd victim died;
And foul contagion spread on ev'ry side;
The helping neighbour, for her kind regard,
Bore home *that* dreadful tribute of reward,
Home, where six children, yielding to its pow'r,
Gave hope and patience a most trying hour;   20
One at her breast still drew the living stream,
And sense of danger never marr'd his dream;
Yet all exclaim'd, and with a pitying eye
'Whoe'er survives the shock, *that child will die!*'
But vain the fiat,—Heav'n restor'd them all,
And destin'd one of riper years to fall.
Midnight beheld the close of all his pain,
His grave was clos'd when midnight came again;
No bell was heard to toll, no funeral pray'r,
No kindred bow'd, no wife, no children there;   30
Its horrid nature could inspire a dread
That cut the bonds of custom like a thread.

Song, Sung by Mr. Bloomfield at the Anniversary of Doctor Jenner's Birth-Day, 1803

Come hither, mild Beauty, that dwell'st on the mountain,
  Sweet handmaid of Liberty, meet us to-day;
Thy votaries philanthropy ask from thy fountain,
  A soul-cheering nectar wherewith to be gay.

The cup may o'erflow, and new grapes still be growing;
  The eyes of the drinkers resplendently shine;
But grant us, bright nymph, with thy gifts overflowing,
  To lighten our hearts, and to relish our wine.

Is Beauty's gay rosebud a prize worth ensuring?
  Its guardianship rests with the friends of our cause.   10
Shall we mark unconcern'd, what the blind are enduring?
  No! mercy and peace are the first of our laws.

Wave, streamers of victory; be bravery requited;
  Be sails, in all climes, still with honour unfurl'd;
All lovers of man with our cause are delighted;
  'Tis to banish the fears, and the tears of the world.

All nations shall feel, and all nations inherit
  The wonderful blessing we place in their view;
And if in that blessing a mortal claims merit,
  Oh! Jenner—your country resigns it to you!   20

From the field, from the farm, comes the glorious treasure,
  May its life-saving impulse—all fresh as the morn—
Still spread round the earth without bounds, without measure,
  Till Time has forgot, when his Jenner was born.

To His Wife (1804)

I rise, dear Mary, from the soundest rest,
A wandering, way-worn, musing, singing guest.
I claim the privilege of hill and plain;
Mine are the woods, and all that they contain;
The unpolluted gale, which sweeps the glade;
All the cool blessings of the solemn shade;
Health, and the flow of happiness sincere;
Yet there's one wish,—I wish that thou wert here;
Free from the trammels of domestic care,
With me these dear autumnal sweets to share;   10
To share my heart's ungovernable joy;
And keep the birth-day of our poor lame boy.
Ah! that's a tender string! Yet since I find
That scenes like these, can soothe the harass'd mind,
Trust me, 'twould set *thy* jaded spirits free,
To wander thus through vales and woods with me.
Thou know'st how much I love to steal away
From noise, from uproar, and the blaze of day;
With double transport would my heart rebound
To lead thee, where the clustering nuts are found;   20
No toilsome efforts would our task demand,
For the brown treasure stoops to meet the hand.
Round the tall hazel, beds of moss appear
In green-swards nibbled by the forest deer,
Sun, and alternate shade; while o'er our heads
The cawing rook his glossy pinions spreads;
The noisy jay, his wild-woods dashing through;
The ring-dove's chorus, and the rustling bough;
The far resounding gate; the kite's shrill scream;
The distant ploughman's halloo to his team.   30
This is the chorus to my soul so dear;
It would delight thee too, wert thou but here:
For we might talk of home, and muse o'er days

Of sad distress, and Heaven's mysterious ways;
Our chequer'd fortunes, with a smile retrace,
And build new hopes upon our infant race;
Pour our thanksgivings forth, and weep the while;
Or pray for blessings on our native isle.
But vain the wish!—Mary, thy sighs forbear,
Nor grudge the pleasure which thou canst not share;   40
Make home delightful, kindly wish for me,
And I'll leave hills, and dales, and woods for thee.
                    Whittlebury Forest, Sept. 16, 1804.

To A Spindle (1805)

The portrait of my mother was taken on her last visit to London, in the summer of 1804, and about six months previous to her dissolution. During the period of evident decline in her strength and faculties, she conceived, in place of that patient resignation which she had before felt, an ungovernable dread of ultimate want; and observed to a relative, with peculiar emphasis, that 'to meet Winter, Old Age, and Poverty, was like meeting three giants.'

To the last hour of her life she was an excellent spinner; and latterly, the peculiar kind of wool she spun, was brought exclusively for her, as being the only one in the village, who exercised their industry on so fine a sort. During the tearful paroxysms of her last depression, she spun with the utmost violence, and with vehemence exclaimed, '*I must spin!*' A paralytic affection, struck her whole right side, while at work, and obliged her to quit her spindle when only half filled, and she died within a fortnight afterwards. I have that spindle now.

She was buried on the last day of the year 1804. She returned from her visit to London, on Friday, the 29th of June, just to a day, 23 years after she brought me to London, which was also on a Friday, in the year 1781.

Relic! I will not bow to thee, nor worship!
Yet, treasure as thou art, remembrancer
Of sunny days, that ever haunt my dreams,
Where thy brown fellows as a task I twirl'd,
And sang my ditties, ere the farm received
My vagrant foot, and with its liberty,
And all its cheerful buds, and op'ning flowers,
Had taught my heart to wander:
—Relic of affection! come;—
Thou shalt a moral teach to me and mine;   10
The hand that wore thee smooth is cold, and spins
No more! Debility press'd hard, around
The seat of life, and terrors fill'd her brain,—
Nor causeless terrors. Giants grim and bold,

Three mighty ones she fear'd to meet:—they came—
Winter, Old Age, and Poverty,—all came;
The last had dropp'd his club, yet fancy made
Him formidable; and when Death beheld
Her tribulation, he fulfill'd his task,
And to her trembling hand and heart at once,   20
Cried, 'Spin no more.'—Thou then wert left half fill'd
With this soft downy fleece, such as she wound
Through all her days, she who could spin so well.
Half fill'd wert thou—half finish'd when she died!
—Half finish'd? 'Tis the motto of the world:
We spin vain threads, and strive, and die
With sillier things than spindles on our hands!

   Then feeling, as I do, resistlessly,
The bias set upon my soul for verse;
Oh, should old age still find my brain at work,   30
And Death, o'er some poor fragment striding, cry
'Hold! spin no more!' grant, Heaven, that purity
Of thought and texture, may assimilate
That fragment unto thee, in usefulness,
In worth, and snowy innocence. Then shall
The village school-mistress, shine brighter through
The exit of her boy; and both shall live,
And virtue triumph too; and virtue's tears,
Like Heaven's pure blessings, fall upon their grave.

From *Wild Flowers; or, Pastoral and Local Poetry* (1806)

Dedication. To My Eldest Son

My Dear Boy,

In thus addressing myself to you, and in expressing my regard for your person, my anxiety for your health, and my devotion to your welfare, I enjoy an advantage over those dedicators who indulge in adulation;—I shall at least be believed.

Should you arrive at that period when reason shall be mature, and affection or curiosity induce you to look back on your father's poetical progress through life, you may conclude that he had many to boast as friends, whose names, in a dedication would have honoured both him and his children; but you must also reflect, that to particularize such friends was a point of peculiar delicacy. The earliest patron of my unprotected strains has the warm thanks which are his due, for the introduction of blessings which have been diffused through our whole family; and nothing will ever change this sentiment. But amidst a general feeling of gratitude, which those who know me will never dispute, I feel for you, Charles, what none but parents can conceive; and on your account, my dear boy, there can be no harm in telling the world that I hope these 'Wild Flowers' will be productive of sweets of the worldly kind; for your unfortunate lameness (should it never be removed) may preclude you from the means of procuring comforts and advantages which might otherwise have fallen to your share.

What a lasting, what an unspeakable satisfaction would it be to know that the Ballads, the Ploughman Stories, and the 'Broken Crutch' of your father would eventually contribute to lighten your steps to manhood, and make your own crutch, through life, rather a memorial of affection, than an object of sorrow.

With a parent's feelings, and a parent's cares and hopes,

I am, Charles, yours,   R.B.

From the Preface to the First Edition

A Man of the first eminence, in whose day (fortunately perhaps for me) I was not destined to appear before the public, or to abide the Herculean crab-tree of his criticism, Dr. Johnson, has said, in his preface to Shakspeare that—'Nothing can please many, and please long, but just representations of general nature.' My representations of nature, whatever may be said of their *justness*, are not *general*, unless we admit, what I suspect to be the case, that nature in a village is very much like nature every where else. It will be observed that all my pictures are from humble life, and most of my heroines servant maids. Such I would have them: being fully persuaded that, in no other way would my endeavours, either to please or to instruct, have an equal chance of success.

The path I have thus taken, from necessity, as well as from choice, is well understood and approved by hundreds, who are capable of ranging in the higher walks of literature.—But with due deference to their superior claim, I confess, that no recompense has been half so grateful or half so agreeable to me as female approbation. To be readily and generally understood, to have my simple Tales almost instinctively relished by those who have so decided an influence over the lives, hearts, and manners of us all, is the utmost stretch of my ambition.

I here venture, before the public eye, a selection from the various pieces which have been the source of much pleasure, and the solace of my leisure hours during the last four years and since the publication of the 'Rural Tales.' Perhaps, in some of them, more of mirth is intermingled than many who know me would expect, or than the severe will be inclined to approve. But surely what I can say, or can be expected to say, on subjects of country life, would gain little by the seriousness of a preacher, or by exhibiting fallacious representations of what has long been termed *Rural Innocence...*

I anticipate some approbation from such readers as have been pleased with the 'Rural Tales;' yet, though I will not falsify my own feelings by assuming a diffidence which I do not conceive to be either manly or becoming, the conviction that some reputation is hazarded in 'a third attempt,' is impressed deeply on my mind.

With such sentiments, and with a lively sense of the high honour, and a hope of the bright recompence, of applause from the good, when heightened by the self-approving voice of my own conscience, I commit the book to its fate.

Robert Bloomfield

TO MY OLD OAK TABLE

Friend of my peaceful days! substantial friend,
Whom wealth can never change, nor int'rest bend,
I love thee like a child. Thou wert to me
The dumb companion of my misery,
And oftner of my joys;—then as I spoke,
I shar'd thy sympathy, Old Heart of Oak!
For surely when my labour ceas'd at night,
With trembling, feverish hands, and aching sight,
The draught that cheer'd me and subdu'd my care,
On thy broad shoulders thou wert proud to bear.   10
O'er thee, with expectation's fire elate,
I've sat and ponder'd on my future fate:
On thee, with winter muffins for thy store,
I've lean'd, and quite forgot that I was poor.
        Where dropp'd the acorn that gave birth to thee?
Can'st thou trace back thy line of ancestry?
We're match'd, old friend, and let us not repine,
Darkness o'erhangs thy origin and mine;
Both may be truly honourable: yet,
We'll date our honours from the day we met;   20
When, of my worldly wealth the parent stock,
Right welcome up the Thames from Woolwich Dock
Thou cam'st, when hopes ran high, and love was young;
But soon our olive-branches round thee sprung;
Soon came the days that tried a faithful wife,
The noise of children, and the cares of life.
Then, midst the threat'nings of a wintry sky,
That cough which blights the bud of infancy,
The dread of parents, Rest's inveterate foe,
Came like a plague, and turn'd my songs to woe.   30
        Rest! without thee what strength can long survive,
What spirit keep the flame of Hope alive?
The midnight murmur of the cradle gave
Sounds of despair; and chilly as the grave
We felt its undulating blast arise,
Midst whisper'd sorrows and ten thousand sighs.
Expiring embers warn'd us each to sleep,
By turns to watch alone, by turns to weep,
By turns to hear, and keep from starting wild,

The sad, faint wailings of a dying child.   40
But Death, obedient to Heav'n's high command,
Withdrew his jav'lin, and unclench'd his hand;
The little sufferers triumph'd over pain,
Their mother smil'd, and bade me hope again.
Yet Care gain'd ground, Exertion triumph'd less,
Thick fell the gathering terrors of Distress;
Anxiety, and Griefs without a name,
Had made their dreadful inroads on my frame;
The creeping Dropsy, cold as cold could be,
Unnerved my arm, and bow'd my head to thee.   50
Thou to thy trust, old friend, hast not been true;
These eyes the bitterest tears they ever knew
Let fall upon thee; now all wip'd away;
But what from memory shall wipe out that day?
The great, the wealthy of my native land,
To whom a guinea is a grain of sand,
I thought upon them, for my *thoughts* were free,
But all unknown were then my woes and me.
    Still, Resignation was my dearest friend,
And Reason pointed to a glorious end;   60
With anxious sighs, a parent's hopes and pride,
I wish'd to live—I trust I could have died!
But winter's clouds pursu'd their stormy way,
And March brought sunshine with the length'ning day,
And bade my heart arise, that morn and night
Now throbb'd with irresistible delight.
Delightful 'twas to leave disease behind,
And feel the renovation of the mind!
To lead abroad, upborne on Pleasure's wing,
Our children, midst the glories of the spring;   70
Our fellow-sufferers, our only wealth,
To gather daisies in the breeze of health!
    'Twas then, too, when our prospects grew so fair,
And Sabbath bells announc'd the morning pray'r;
Beneath that vast gigantic dome we bow'd,
That lifts its flaming cross above the cloud;
Had gain'd the centre of the chequer'd floor;—
That instant, with reverberating roar
Burst forth the pealing organ—mute we stood;—

The strong sensation boiling through my blood,   80
Rose in a storm of joy, allied to pain,
I wept, and worshipp'd God, and wept again;
And felt, amidst the fervor of my praise,
The sweet assurances of better days.
    In that gay season, honest friend of mine,
I marked the brilliant sun upon thee shine;
Imagination took her flights so free,
Home was delicious with my book and thee,
The purchas'd nosegay, or brown ears of corn,
Were thy gay plumes upon a summer's morn,   90
Awakening memory, that disdains control,
They spoke the darling language of my soul:
They whisper'd tales of joy, of peace, of truth,
And conjur'd back the sunshine of my youth:
Fancy presided at the joyful birth,
I pour'd the torrent of my feelings forth;
Conscious of *truth* in Nature's humble track,
And wrote 'The Farmer's Boy' upon thy back!
Enough, old friend:—thou'rt mine; and shalt partake,
While I have pen to write, or tongue to speak,   100
Whatever fortune deals me.—Part with thee!
No, not till death shall set my spirit free;
For know, should plenty crown my life's decline,
A most important duty may be thine:
Then, guard me from Temptation's base control,
From apathy and littleness of soul.
The sight of thy old frame, so rough, so rude,
Shall twitch the sleeve of nodding Gratitude;
Shall teach me but to venerate the more
Honest Oak Tables and their guests—the poor;   110
Teach me unjust distinctions to deride,
And falsehoods gender'd in the brain of Pride;
Shall give to Fancy still the cheerful hour,
To Intellect, its freedom and its power;
To Hospitality's enchanting ring
A charm, which nothing but thyself can bring.
The man who would not look with honest pride
On the tight bark that stemm'd the roaring tide,
And bore him, when he bow'd the trembling knee,

Home, through the mighty perils of the sea,   120
I love him not.—He ne'er shall be my guest;
Nor sip my cup, nor witness how I'm blest;
Nor lean, to bring my honest friend to shame,
A sacrilegious elbow on thy frame;
But thou through life a monitor shalt prove,
Sacred to Truth, to Poetry, and Love.
                    Dec. 1803.

THE HORKEY. A PROVINCIAL BALLAD

Advertisement

In the descriptive ballad which follows, it will be evident that I have endeavoured to preserve the style of a gossip, and to transmit the memorial of a custom, the extent or antiquity of which I am not acquainted with, and pretend not to inquire.

In Suffolk husbandry the man who, (whether by merit or by sufferance I know not) goes foremost through the harvest with the scythe or the sickle, is honoured with the title of 'Lord,' and at the Horkey, or harvest-home feast, collects what he can, for himself and brethren, from the farmers and visitors, to make a 'frolic' afterwards, called 'the largess spending.' By way of returning thanks, though perhaps formerly of much more, or of different signification, they immediately leave the seat of festivity, and with a very long and repeated shout of a 'largess' (the number of shouts being regulated by the sums given) seem to wish to make themselves heard by the people of the surrounding farms. And before they rejoin the company within, the pranks and the jollity I have endeavoured to describe, usually take place. These customs, I believe, are going fast out of use; which is one great reason for my trying to tell the rising race of mankind that such were the customs when I was a boy.

I have annexed a glossary of such words as may be found by general readers to require explanation: And will add a short extract from Sir Thomas Brown, of Norwich, M. D. who was born three years before Milton, and outlived him eight years:

'It were not impossible to make an original reduction of many words of no general reception in *England*, but of common use in *Norfolk*, or peculiar to the *East-Angle* counties; as Bawnd, Bunny, Thurck, Enemis, Matchly, Sammodithee, Mawther, Kedge, Seele, Straft, Clever, Dere, Nicked, Stingy, Noneare, Feft, Thepes, Gosgood, Kamp, Sibrit, Fangast, Sap, Cothish, Thokish, Bide-owe, Paxwax. Of these, and some others, of no easy originals, when time will permit, the resolution shall be attempted; which to effect, the Danish language, new, and more ancient, may prove of good advantage: which nation remained here fifty years upon agreement, and have left many families in it; and the language of these parts had surely been more commixed and perplex, if the fleet of *Hugo de Bones* had not been cast away, wherein threescore thousand souldiers, out of Britany and Flanders, were to be wafted over, and were, by King *John*'s appointment, to have a settled habitation in the counties of *Norfolk* and *Suffolk*.'—Tract the viii. on Languages, particularly the Saxon Folio, 1686, p. 48.

I

What gossips prattled in the sun,
    Who talk'd him fairly down,
Up, Memory! tell; 'tis Suffolk fun,
    And lingo of their own.

II

Ah! *Judie Twitchet!* though thou'rt dead,
    With thee the tale begins;
For still seems thrumming in my head
    The rattling of thy pins.

III

Thou Queen of knitters! for a ball
    Of worsted was thy pride;
With dangling stockings great and small,
    And world of clack beside!

10

IV

'We did so laugh; the moon shone bright;
    More fun you never knew;
'Twas Farmer Cheerum's *Horkey night*,
    And I, and Grace, and Sue—

V

But bring a stool, sit round about,
    And boys, be quiet, pray;
And let me tell my story out;
    'Twas *sitch* a merry day!   20

VI

The butcher whistled at the door,
    And brought a load of meat;
Boys rubb'd their hands, and cried, "there's more,"
    Dogs wagg'd their tails to see't.

VII

On went the boilers till the *hake*
    Had much ado to bear 'em;
The magpie talk'd for talking sake,
    Birds sung;—but who could hear 'em?

VIII

Creak went the jack; the cats were *scar'd*,
    We had not time to heed 'em,   30
The *owd hins* cackled in the yard,
    For we forgot to feed 'em!

IX

Yet 'twas not I, as I may say,
    Because as how, d'ye see,
I only help'd there for the day;
    They cou'dn't lay't to me.

X

Now Mrs. Cheerum's best lace cap
    Was mounted on her head;
Guests at the door began to rap,
    And now the cloth was spread.   40

XI

Then clatter went the earthen plates—
    "Mind, Judie," was the cry;
I could have *cop't* them at their pates;
    "Trenchers for me," said I,

XII

That look so clean upon the ledge,
    All proof against a fall;
They never turn a sharp knife's edge,
    But fashion rules us all.

XIII

Home came the jovial *Horkey load,*
    Last of the whole year's crop;   50
And Grace amongst the green boughs rode
    Right plump upon the top.

XIV

This way and that the waggon reel'd,
    And never queen rode higher;
Her cheeks were colour'd in the fields,
    And ours before the fire.

XV

The laughing harvest-folks, and John,
    Came in and look'd askew;
'Twas my red face that set them on,
    And then they leer'd at Sue.   60

XVI

And Farmer Cheerum went, good man,
    And broach'd the *Horkey beer;*
And *sitch a mort* of folks began
    To eat up our good cheer.

XVII

Says he, "Thank God for what's before us;
    That thus we meet agen;"
The mingling voices, like a chorus,
    Join'd cheerfully, "Amen."—

XVIII

Welcome and plenty, there they found 'em,
    The ribs of beef grew light;   70
And puddings—till the boys got round 'em,
    And then they vanish'd quite.

XIX

Now all the guests, with Farmer Crouder,
    Began to prate of corn;
And we found out they talk'd the louder,
    The oftner pass'd the Horn.

XX

Out came the nuts; we set a cracking;
    The ale came round our way;
By gom, we women fell a clacking
    As loud again as they.   80

XXI

John sung "Old Benbow" loud and strong,
    And I, "The Constant Swain,"
"Cheer up, my Lads," was Simon's song,
    "We'll conquer them again."

XXII

Now twelve o'clock was drawing nigh,
    And all in merry cue;
I knock'd the cask, "O, ho!" said I,
    "We've almost conquer'd you."

XXIII

My Lord begg'd round, and held his hat,
    Says Farmer Gruff, says he,   90
"There's many a Lord, Sam, I know that,
    Has begg'd as well as thee."

XXIV

Bump in his hat the shillings tumbled
    All round among the folks;
"Laugh if you wool," said Sam, and mumbled,
    "You pay for all your jokes."

XXV

Joint stock you know among the men,
 To drink at their own charges;
So up they got full drive, and then
 Went out to *halloo largess*.   100

XXVI

And sure enough the noise they made!!—
 —But let me mind my tale:
We follow'd them, we worn't afraid,
 We 'ad all been drinking ale.

XXVII

As they stood hallooing back to back,
 We, lightly as a feather,
Went sideling round, and in a crack
 Had pinn'd their coats together.

XXVIII

'Twas near upon't as light as noon;
 A largess, on the hill,   110
They shouted to the full round moon,
 I think I hear 'em still!

XXIX

But when they found the trick, my stars!
 They well knew who to blame,
Our giggles turn'd to loud ha, ha's,
 And *arter* us they came.

XXX

The hindmost was the dairy-maid,
 And Sam came blundering by;
She could not shun him, so they said;
 I *know* she did not try.   120

XXXI

And off set John, with all his might,
 To chase me down the yard,
Till I was nearly *gran'd* outright;
 He hugg'd so woundy hard.

XXXII

Still they kept up the race and laugh,
 And round the house we flew;
But hark ye! the best fun by half
 Was Simon *arter* Sue.

XXXIII

She car'd not, dark nor light, not she,
 So, near the dairy door   130
She pass'd a clean white hog, you see,
 They'd *kilt* the day before.

XXXIV

High on the *spirket* there it hung,—
 "Now, Susie—what can save ye?"
Round the cold pig his arms he flung,
 And cried, "Ah! here I have ye!"

XXXV

The farmers heard what Simon said,
 And what a noise! good lack!
Some almost laugh'd themselves *to dead*
 And others clapt his back.   140

XXXVI

We all at once began to tell
 What fun we had abroad;
But Simon stood our jeers right well;
 —He fell asleep and snor'd.

XXXVII

Then in his button-hole upright,
 Did Farmer Crouder put
A slip of paper, twisted tight,
 And held the candle *to't*.

XXXVIII

It smok'd, and smok'd, beneath his nose,
 The harmless blaze crept higher; 150
Till with a vengeance up he rose,
 Fire, Judie, Sue! fire, fire!

XXXIX

The clock struck one—some talk'd of parting,
    Some said it was a sin,
And *hitch'd* their chairs;—but those for starting
    Now let the moonlight in.

XL

Owd women, loitering *for the nonce*,
    Stood praising the fine weather;
The menfolks took the hint at once
    To kiss them altogether.   160

XLI

And out ran every soul beside,
    A *shanny-pated* crew;
Owd folks could neither run nor hide,
    So some *ketch'd* one, some *tew*.

XLII

They *skriggl'd* and began to scold,
    But laughing got the master;
Some *quack'ling* cried, "let go your hold;"
    The farmers held the faster.

XLIII

All innocent, that I'll be sworn,
    There worn't a bit of sorrow,   170
And women, if their gowns *are* torn,
    Can mend them on the morrow.

XLIV

Our shadows helter skelter danc'd
    About the moonlight ground;
The wondering sheep, as on we pranc'd,
    Got up and gaz'd around.

XLV

And well they might—till Farmer Cheerum,
    Now with a hearty glee,
Bade all good morn as he came near 'em,
    And then to bed went he.   180

XLVI

Then off we stroll'd this way and that,
    With merry voices ringing;
And Echo answered us right pat,
    As home we rambl'd singing.

XLVII

For, when we laugh'd, it laugh'd again,
    And to our own doors follow'd!
"Yo, ho!" we cried; "Yo, ho!" so plain,
    The misty meadow halloo'd.

XLVIII

That's all my tale, and all the fun,
    Come, turn your wheels about;   190
My worsted, see! that's nicely done,
    Just held my story out!!'

XLIX

Poor Judie!—Thus Time knits or spins
    The worsted from Life's ball!
Death stopt thy tales, and stopt thy pins,
    —And so he'll serve us all.

THE BROKEN CRUTCH. A TALE

'I tell you, Peggy,' said a voice behind
A hawthorn hedge, with wild briars thick entwin'd,
Where unseen trav'llers down a shady way
Journey'd beside the swaths of new-mown hay,
'I tell you, Peggy, 'tis a time to prove
Your fortitude, your virtue, and your love.
From honest poverty our lineage sprung,
Your mother was a servant quite as young;—
You weep; perhaps *she* wept at leaving home;
Courage, my girl, nor fear the days to come.   10
Go still to church, my Peggy, plainly drest,
And keep a living conscience in your breast;
Look to yourself, my lass, the maid's best fame,
Beware, nor bring the Meldrums into shame:
Be modest, to the voice of truth attend,
Be honest, and you'll always find a friend:

Your uncle Gilbert, stronger far than I,
Will see you safe; on him you must rely:
I've walk'd too far; this lameness, oh! the pain;
Heav'n bless thee, child! I'll halt me back again;   20
But when your first fair holiday may be,
Do, dearest Peggy, spend your hours with me.'
    Young Herbert Brooks, in strength and manhood bold,
Who, round the meads, his own possessions, stroll'd,
O'erheard the charge, and with a heart so gay,
Whistled his spaniel, and pursu'd his way.
Soon cross'd his path, and short obeisance paid,
Stout Gilbert Meldrum and a country maid;
A box upon his shoulder held full well
Her worldly riches, but the truth to tell   30
She bore the chief herself; that nobler part,
That beauteous gem, an uncorrupted heart.
And then that native loveliness! that cheek!
It bore the very tints her betters seek.
At such a sight the libertine would glow
With all the warmth that *he* can never know;
Would send his thoughts abroad without control,
The glimmering moonshine of his little soul.
'Above the reach of justice I shall soar,
Her friends may rail, not punish; they're too poor: 40
That very thought the rapture will enhance,
Poor, young, and friendless; what a glorious chance!
A few spare guineas may the conquest make,—
I love the treachery for treachery's sake,—
And when her wounded honour jealous grows,
I'll cut away ten thousand oaths and vows,
And bravely boast, all snarling fools defying,
How I, *a girl out-witted*,—just by lying.'
Such was not Herbert—he had never known
Love's genuine smiles, nor suffer'd from his frown;   50
And as to that most honourable part
Of planting daggers in a parent's heart,
A novice quite:—he past his hours away,
Free as a bird, and buxom as the day;
Yet, should a lovely girl by chance arise,
Think not that Herbert Brooks would shut his eyes.

On thy calm joys with what delight I dream,
Thou dear green valley of my native stream!
Fancy o'er thee still waves th'enchanting wand,
And every nook of thine is fairy land,　　　　　　　60
And ever will be, though the axe should smite
In Gain's rude service, and in Pity's spite,
Thy clustering alders, and at length invade
The last, last poplars, that compose thy shade:
Thy stream shall still in native freedom stray,
And undermine the willows in its way,
These, nearly worthless, may survive this storm,
This scythe of desolation call'd 'Reform.'
No army past that way! yet are they fled,
The boughs that, when a school-boy, screen'd my head:　70
I hate the murderous axe; estranging more
The winding vale from what it was of yore,
Than e'en mortality in all its rage,
And all the change of faces in an age.
'Warmth,' will they term it, that I speak so free;
They strip thy shades,—thy shades so dear to me!
In Herbert's days woods cloth'd both hill and dale;
But peace, Remembrance! let us tell the tale.
　　　　His home was in the valley, elms grew round
His moated mansion, and the pleasant sound　　　　80
Of woodland birds that loud at day-break sing,
With the first cuckoos that proclaim the spring,
Flock'd round his dwelling; and his kitchen smoke,
That from the towering rookery upward broke,
Of joyful import to the poor hard by,
Stream'd a glad sign of hospitality;
So fancy pictures; but its day is o'er;
The moat remains; the dwelling is no more!
Its name denotes its melancholy fall,
For village children call the spot 'Burnt-Hall.'　　　90
　　　　But where's the maid, who in the meadow-way
Met Herbert Brooks amongst the new-mown hay?
　　　　Th'adventure charm'd him, and next morning rose
The Sabbath, with its silence and repose;
The bells ceas'd chiming, and the broad blue sky
Smil'd on his peace, and met his tranquil eye

Inverted, from the foot-bridge on his way
To that still house where all his fathers lay;
There in his seat, each neighbour's face he knew—
The stranger girl was just before his pew!   100
He saw her kneel, with meek, but cheerful air,
And whisper the response to every prayer;
And, when the humble roof with praises rung,
He caught the Hallelujah from her tongue,
Rememb'ring with delight the tears that fell
When the poor father bade his child farewell;
And now, by kindling tenderness beguil'd,
He blest the prompt obedience of that child,
And link'd his fate with hers:—for, from that day,
Whether the weeks past cheerily away,   110
Or deep revolving doubts procur'd him pain,
The same bells chim'd—and there she was again!
What could be done? they came not there to woo,
On holy ground,—though love is holy too.
      They met upon the foot-bridge one clear morn,
She in the garb by village lasses worn;
He, with unbutton'd frock that careless flew,
And buskin'd to resist the morning dew;
With downcast look she courtsied to the ground,
Just in his path—no room to sidle round.   120
      'Well, pretty girl, this early rising yields
The best enjoyment of the groves and fields.
And makes the heart susceptible and meek,
And keeps alive that rose upon your cheek.
I long'd to meet you, Peggy, though so shy,
I've watch'd your steps, and learn'd your history;
You love your poor lame father, let that be
A happy presage of your love for me.
Come then, I'll stroll these meadows by your side,
I've seen enough to wish you for my bride,   130
And I *must* tell you so.—Nay, let me hold
This guiltless hand, I prize it more than gold;
Of that I have my share, but fain would prove
The sterling wealth of honourable love;
My lands are fruitful, and my flocks increase,
My house knows plenty, and my servants peace;

One blessing more will crown my happy life,
Like Adam, pretty girl, I want a wife.'
   Need it be told his suit was not denied,
With youth, and wealth, and candour on his side?   140
Honour took charge of love so well begun,
And accidental meetings, one by one,
Increas'd so fast midst time's unheeded flight,
That village rumour married them outright;
Though wiser matrons, doubtful in debate,
Pitied deluded Peggy's hapless fate.
Friends took th'alarm, 'And will he then disgrace
The name of Brooks with this plebeian race?'
Others, more lax in virtue, not in pride,
Sported the wink of cunning on one side;   150
'He'll buy, no doubt, what Peggy has to sell,
A little gallantry becomes him well.'
Meanwhile the youth, with self-determin'd aim,
Disdaining fraud, and pride's unfeeling claim,
Above control, pursued his generous way,
And talk'd to Peggy of the marriage-day.
Poor girl! she heard, with anguish and with doubt,
What her too-knowing neighbours preach'd about,
That Herbert would some nobler match prefer,
And surely never, never marry her;   160
Yet, with what trembling and delight she bore
The kiss, and heard the vow, 'I'll doubt no more;
Protect me, Herbert, for your honour's sake
You will,' she cried, 'nor leave my heart to break.'
Then wrote to uncle Gilbert, joys, and fears,
And hope, and trust, and sprinkled all with tears.
   Rous'd was the dormant spirit of the brave,
E'en lameness rose to succour and to save;
For, though they both rever'd young Herbert's name,
And knew his unexceptionable fame;   170
And though the girl had honestly declar'd
Love's first approaches, and their counsel shar'd,
Yet, that he truly meant to take for life
The poor and lowly Peggy for a wife;
Or, that she was not doom'd to be deceiv'd,
Was out of bounds:—it *could not* be believ'd.

'Go, Gilbert, save her; I, you know, am lame;
Go, brother, go, and save my child from shame.
Haste, and I'll pray for your success the while,
Go, go;' then bang'd his crutch upon the stile:—   180
It snapt.—E'en Gilbert trembled while he smote,
Then whipt the broken end beneath his coat;
'Aye, aye, I'll settle them; I'll let them see
Who's to be conqu'ror this time, I or he!'
    Then off he set, and with enormous strides,
Rebellious mutterings and oaths besides,
O'er cloverfield and fallow, bank and briar,
Pursu'd the nearest cut, and fann'd the fire
That burnt within him.—Soon the Hall he spied,
And the grey willows by the water side;   190
Nature cried 'halt!' nor could he well refuse;
Stop, Gilbert, breathe awhile, and ask *the news*.
'News?' cried a stooping grandame of the vale,
'Aye, rare news too; I'll tell you such a tale;
But let me rest; this bank is dry and warm;
Do you know Peggy Meldrum at the farm?
Young Herbert's girl? He'as cloth'd her all in white,
You never saw so beautiful a sight!
Ah! he's a fine young man, and such a face!
I knew his grandfather and all his race;   200
He rode a tall white horse, and look'd so big,
But how shall I describe his hat and wig?'
'Plague take his wig,' cried Gilbert, 'and his hat,
Where's Peggy Meldrum? can you tell me *that?*
'Aye; but have patience, man! you'll hear anon,
For I shall come to her as I go on,
So hark'ye friend; his grandfather I say,'—
'Poh, poh,'—cried Gilbert, as he turn'd away.
Her eyes were fix'd, her story at a stand,
The snuff-box lay half open'd in her hand;   210
'You great, ill-manner'd clown! but I must bear it;
You oaf; to ask the news, and then won't hear it!'
But Gilbert had gain'd forty paces clear,
When the reproof came murmuring on his ear.
    Again he ask'd the first that pass'd him by;
A cow-boy stopt his whistle to reply.

'Why, I've a mistress coming home, that's all,
They're playing Meg's diversion at the Hall;
For master's gone, with Peggy, and his cousin,
And all the lady-folks, about a dozen,   220
To church, down there; he'll marry *one* no doubt,
For that it seems is what they're gone about;
I know it by their laughing and their jokes,
Tho' they *wor'nt* ask'd at church like other folks.'
    Gilbert kept on, and at the Hall-door found
The winking servants, where the jest went round:
All expectation; aye, and so was he,
But not with heart so merry and so free.
The kitchen table, never clear from beef,
Where hunger found its solace and relief,   230
Free to all strangers, had no charms for him,
For agitation worried every limb;
Ale he partook, but appetite had none,
And grey-hounds watch'd in vain to catch the bone.
All sounds alarm'd him, and all thoughts perplex'd,
With dogs, and beef, himself, and all things vex'd,
Till with one mingled caw above his head,
Their gliding shadows o'er the court-yard spread,
The rooks by thousands rose: the bells struck up;
He guess'd the cause, and down he set the cup,   240
And listening, heard, amidst the general hum,
A joyful exclamation, 'Here they come!'—
Soon Herbert's cheerful voice was heard above,
Amidst the rustling hand-maids of his love,
And Gilbert follow'd without thought or dread,
The broad oak stair-case thunder'd with his tread;
Light tript the party, gay as gay could be,
Amidst their bridal dresses—there came he!
And with a look that guilt could ne'er withstand,
Approach'd his niece and caught her by the hand,   250
'Now are you married, Peggy, yes or no?
Tell me at once, before I let you go!'
Abrupt he spoke, and gave her arm a swing,
But the same moment felt the wedding ring,
And stood confus'd.—She wip'd th'empassion'd tear,
'I am, I am; but is my father here?'

Herbert stood by, and sharing with his bride,
That perturbation which she strove to hide;
'Come, honest Gilbert, you're too rough this time,
Indeed here's not the shadow of a crime;   260
But where's your brother? When did you arrive?
We waited long, for Nathan went at five!'
      All this was Greek to Gilbert, downright Greek;
He knew not what to think, nor how to speak.
The case was this; that Nathan with a cart
To fetch them both at day-break was to start.
And so he did—but ere he could proceed,
He suck'd a charming portion with a reed,
Of that same wedding-ale, which was that day
To make the hearts of all the village gay;   270
Brim full of glee he trundled from the Hall,
And as for sky-larks, he out-sung them all;
Till growing giddy with his morning cup,
He, stretch'd beneath a hedge, the reins gave up;
The horse graz'd soberly without mishap,
And Nathan had a most delightful nap
For three good hours—Then, doubting, when he woke,
Whether his conduct would be deem'd a joke,
With double haste perform'd just half his part,
And brought the lame John Meldrum in his cart.   280
And at the moment Gilbert's wrath was high,
And while young Herbert waited his reply,
The sound of rattling wheels was at the door;
'There's my dear father now,'—they heard no more,
The bridegroom glided like an arrow down,
And Gilbert ran, though something of a clown,
With his best step; and cheer'd with smiles and pray'rs,
They bore old John in triumph up the stairs:
Poor Peggy, who her joy no more could check,
Clung like a dewy woodbine round his neck.   290
And all stood silent—Gilbert, off his guard,
And marvelling at virtue's rich reward,
Loos'd the one loop that held his coat before,
Down thumpt the broken crutch upon the floor!
They started, half alarm'd, scarce knowing why,
But through the glist'ning rapture of his eye

The bridegroom smil'd, then chid their simple fears,
And rous'd the blushing Peggy from her tears;
Around the uncle in a ring they came,
And mark'd his look of mingled pride and shame.   300
    'Now honestly, good Gilbert, tell us true,
What meant this cudgel? What was it to do?
I know your heart suspected me of wrong,
And that most true affection urg'd along
Your feelings and your wrath; you were beside
Till now the rightful guardian of the bride.
But why this cudgel?'—'Guardian! that's the case,
Or else to-day I had not seen this place,
But John about the girl was so perplex'd,
And I, to tell the truth, so mortal vex'd,   310
That when he broke *this crutch*, and stampt and cried,
For John and Peggy, Sir, I could have died,
Aye, that I could; for she was such a child,
So tractable, so sensible, so mild,
That if between you roguery had grown
(Begging your pardon,) 'twould have been your own;
She would not hurt a fly.—So off I came,
And had I found you injuring her fame,
And base enough to act as hundreds would,
To ruin a poor maid because you *could*,   320
With this same cudgel, (you may smile or frown)
An' please you, Sir, I meant to knock you down.'
    A burst of laughter rang throughout the Hall,
And Peggy's tongue, though overborne by all,
Pour'd its warm blessings; for, without control
The sweet unbridled transport of her soul
Was obviously seen, till Herbert's kiss
Stole, as it were, the eloquence of bliss.
'Welcome, my friends; good Gilbert, here's my hand;
Eat, drink, or rest, they're all at your command: 330
And whatsoever pranks the rest may play,
You still shall be the hero of the day,
Doubts might torment, and blunders may have teaz'd,
Let my ale cure them; let us all be pleas'd.
And as for honest John, let me defend
The father of my new, my bosom friend;

You broke your crutch, well, well, worse luck might be,
I'll be your crutch, John Meldrum, lean on me,
And when your lovely daughter shall complain,
Send Gilbert's wooden argument again.   340
You still may wonder that I take a wife
From the secluded walks of humble life,
On reason's solid ground my love began,
And let the wise confute it if they can.
A girl I saw, with nature's untaught grace,
Turn from my gaze a most engaging face;
I saw her drop the tear, I knew full well
She felt for *you* much more than she could tell.
I found her understanding, bright as day,
Through all impediments still forc'd its way;   350
On that foundation shall my hopes rely,
The rock of genuine humility.
Call'd as she is to act a nobler part,
To rule my household, and to share my heart,
I trust her prudence, confident to prove
Days of delight, and still unfading love;
And, while her inborn tenderness survives,
That heav'nly charm of mothers and of wives,
I'll look for joy:—But see, the neighbours all
Come posting on to share the festival;   360
And I'm determin'd, while the sun's so bright,
That this shall be a wedding-day outright:
How cheerly sound the bells! my charmer, come,
Partake their joy, and know yourself at home.
Sit down, good John;'—'I will,' the old man cried,
'And let me drink to you, Sir, and the bride;
My blessing on you: I am lame and old,
I can't make speeches, and I wo'n't be bold;
But from my soul I wish and wish again,
That brave good gentlemen would not disdain   370
The poor, because they're poor: for, if they live
Midst crimes that parents *never can* forgive,
If, like the forest beast, they wander wild,
To rob a father, or to crush a child,
Nature *will* speak, aye, just as Nature feels,
And wish—a Gilbert Meldrum at their heels.'

SHOOTER'S HILL

Sickness may be often an incentive to poetical composition; I found it so; and I esteem the following lines only because they remind me of past feelings, which I would not willingly forget.

I

Health! I seek thee;—dost thou love
    The mountain-top or quiet vale,
Or deign o'er humbler hills to rove
    On showery June's dark south-west gale?
If so, I'll meet all blasts that blow,
    With silent step, but not forlorn;
Though, goddess, at thy shrine I bow,
    And woo thee each returning morn.

II

I seek thee where, with all his might,
    The joyous bird his rapture tells,   10
Amidst the half-excluded light,
    That gilds the fox-glove's pendant bells;
Where cheerly up the bold hill's side
    The deep'ning groves triumphant climb;
In groves Delight and Peace abide,
    And Wisdom marks the lapse of time.

III

To hide me from the public eye,
    To keep the throne of Reason clear,
Amidst fresh air to breathe or die,
    I took my staff and wander'd here: 20
Suppressing every sigh that heaves,
    And coveting no wealth but thee,
I nestle in the honied leaves,
    And hug my stolen liberty.

IV

O'er eastward uplands, gay or rude,
    Along to Erith's ivied spire,
I start, with strength and hope renew'd,
    And cherish life's rekindling fire.
Now measure vales with straining eyes,
    Now trace the church-yard's humble names;   30
Or, climb brown heaths, abrupt that rise,
    And overlook the winding Thames.

V

I love to mark the flow'ret's eye,
    To rest where pebbles form my bed,
Where shapes and colours scatter'd lie,
    In varying millions round my head.
The soul rejoices when alone,
    And feels her glorious empire free;
Sees God in every shining stone,
    And revels in variety.   40

VI

Ah me! perhaps within my sight,
    Deep in the smiling dales below,
Gigantic talents, Heav'n's pure light,
    And all the rays of genius glow
In some lone soul? whom no one sees
    With power and will to say 'Arise,'
Or chase away the slow disease,
    And Want's foul picture from his eyes.

VII

A worthier man by far than I,
    With more of industry and fire,   50
Shall see fair Virtue's meed pass by,
    Without one spark of fame expire!
Bleed not my heart, it will be so,
    The throb of care was thine full long;
Rise, like the Psalmist from his woe,
    And pour abroad the joyful song.

VIII

Sweet Health, I seek thee! hither bring
    Thy balm that softens human ills;
Come, on the long drawn clouds that fling
    Their shadows o'er the Surry-Hills.   60
Yon green-topt hills, and far away
    Where late as now I freedom stole,
And spent one dear delicious day
    On thy wild banks, romantic *Mole*.

IX

Aye, there's the scene! beyond the sweep
    Of London's congregated cloud,
The dark-brow'd wood, the headlong steep,
    And valley-paths without a crowd!
Here, Thames, I watch thy flowing tides,
    Thy thousand sails am proud to see;   70
But where the *Mole* all silent glides
    Dwells Peace—and Peace is wealth to me!

X

Of Cambrian mountains still I dream,
    And mouldering vestiges of war;
By time-worn cliff or classic stream
    Would rove,—but prudence holds a bar.
Come then, O Health! I'll strive to bound
    My wishes to this airy stand;
'Tis not for *me* to trace around
    The wonders of my native land.   80

XI

Yet, the loud torrent's dark retreat,
    Yet Grampian hills shall Fancy give,
And, towering in her giddy seat,
    Amidst her own creation live,
Live, if thou'lt urge my climbing feet,
    Give strength of nerve and vigorous breath,
If not, with dauntless soul I meet
    The deep solemnity of death.

XII

This far-seen monumental tower
    Records th'achievements of the brave,   90
And Angria's subjugated power,
    Who plunder'd on the eastern wave.
I would not that such turrets rise
    To point out where my bones are laid;
Save that some wandering bard might prize
    The comfort of its broad cool shade.

XIII

O Vanity! since thou'rt decreed
    Companion of our lives to be,
I'll seek the moral songster's meed,
    An earthly immortality;   100
Most vain!—O let me, from the past
    Remembering what to man is given,
Lay Virtue's broad foundations fast,
    Whose glorious turrets reach to Heav'n.

BARNHAM WATER

On a sultry afternoon, late in the summer of 1802, Euston-Hall lay in my way to Thetford, which place I did not reach until the evening, on a visit to my sister: the lines lose much of their interest except they could be read on the spot, or at least at a corresponding season of the year.

I

Fresh from the Hall of Bounty sprung,
    With glowing heart and ardent eye,
With song and rhyme upon my tongue,
    And fairy visions dancing by,
The mid-day sun in all his pow'r
    The backward valley painted gay;
Mine was a road without a flower,
    Where one small streamlet cross'd the way.

II

What was it rous'd my soul to love?
    What made the simple brook so dear?   10
It glided like the weary dove,
    And never brook seem'd half so clear.
Cool pass'd the current o'er my feet,
    Its shelving brink for rest was made,
But every charm was incomplete,
    For Barnham Water wants a shade.

III

There, faint beneath the fervid sun,
    I gaz'd in ruminating mood;
For who can see the current run
    And snatch no feast of mental food?   20
'Keep pure thy soul,' it seem'd to say,
    'Keep that fair path by wisdom trod,
That thou may'st hope to wind thy way,
    To fame worth boasting, and to God.'

IV

Long and delightful was the dream,
    A waking dream that Fancy yields,
Till with regret I left the stream,
    And plung'd across the barren fields;
To where of old rich abbeys smil'd
    In all the pomp of gothic taste,   30
By fond tradition proudly styl'd
    The mighty 'City in the East.'

V

Near, on a slope of burning sand,
    The shepherd boys had met to play,
To hold the plains at their command,
    And mark the trav'ller's leafless way.
The trav'ller with a cheerful look
    Would every pining thought forbear,
If boughs but shelter'd Barnham brook
    He'd stop and leave his blessing there.   40

VI

The Danish mounds of partial green,
    Still, as each mouldering tower decays,
Far o'er the bleak unwooded scene
    Proclaim their wond'rous length of days.
My burning feet, my aching sight,
    Demanded rest—why did I weep?
The moon arose, and such a night!
    Good Heav'n! it was a sin to sleep.

VII

All rushing came thy hallow'd sighs,
    Sweet Melancholy, from my breast;   50
"Tis here that eastern greatness lies,
    That Might, Renown, and Wisdom rest!
Here funeral rites the priesthood gave
    To chiefs who sway'd prodigious powers,
The Bigods and the Mowbrays brave,
    From Framlingham's imperial towers.'

VIII

Full of the mighty deeds of yore,
    I bade good night the trembling beam;
Fancy e'en heard the battle's roar,
    Of what but slaughter could I dream?   60
Bless'd be that night, that trembling beam,
    Peaceful excursions Fancy made;
All night I heard the bubbling stream,
    Yet, Barnham Water wants a shade.

IX

Whatever hurts my country's fame,
    When wits and mountaineers deride,
To me grows serious, for I name
    My native plains and streams with pride.
No mountain charms have I to sing,
    No loftier minstrel's rights invade;   70
From trifles oft *my* raptures spring;
    —Sweet Barnham Water wants a shade.

From *The Banks of Wye* (1811)

Preface

In the summer of 1807, a party of my good friends in Gloucestershire, proposed to themselves a short excursion down the Wye, and through part of South Wales.

While this plan was in agitation, the lines which I had composed on 'Shooter's Hill,' during ill health, and inserted in my last volume, obtained their particular attention. A spirit of prediction, as well as sorrow, is there indulged; and it was now in the power of this happy party to falsify such predictions, and to render a pleasure to the writer of no common kind. An invitation to accompany them was the consequence; and the following Journal is the result of that invitation.

Should the reader, from being a resident, or frequent visitor, be well acquainted with the route, and able to discover inaccuracies in distances, succession of objects, or local particulars, he is requested to recollect, that the party was out but ten days; a period much too short for correct and laborious description, but quite sufficient for all the powers of poetry which I feel capable of exerting. The whole exhibits the language and feelings of a man who had never before seen a mountainous country; and of this it is highly necessary that the reader should be apprized.

A Swiss, or perhaps a Scottish Highlander, may smile at supposed or real exaggerations; but they will be excellent critics, when they call to mind that they themselves judge, in these cases, as I do, by comparison.

Perhaps it may be said, that because much of public approbation has fallen to my lot, it was unwise to venture again. I confess that the journey left such powerful, such unconquerable impressions on my mind, that embodying my thoughts in rhyme became a matter almost of necessity. To the parties concerned I know it will be an acceptable little volume: to whom, and to the public, it is submitted with due respect.

Robert Bloomfield. City Road, London, June 30, 1811

Advertisement to the Second Edition (1813)

When this Poem, or Journal, was submitted to the Public, I endeavoured to meet that confined and temporary approbation, which its locality induced me to expect. It is, therefore, with no small pleasure that I have, thus, in a Second Edition, the power of correcting, and I hope amending, this favourite of my fancy, this gem of my memory, which flashes upon me still like the sunshine of Spring.

I have seen no regular critique on the piece, strange as it may appear, (for I have left London,) and consequently, in the present instance, have not the advantage of public criticism.

The Lady whose name appears in the Dedication [Mrs. Lloyd Baker] is no more; she was a wife and a mother, in their truest sense. And, it is sufficient for me to say, that she possessed the character which distinguishes her uncle, the venerable Granville Sharp.

In my own family, I have sustained the loss of my second daughter, in her twentieth year; yet, while Providence grants me peace of mind, I enjoy repose, and am, the Reader's Obedient, R.B.

Shefford, Beds, April 7, 1813.

FROM *JOURNAL OF A TOUR DOWN THE WYE* [1807]
[The ascent of the Sugar-Loaf, Abergavenny]

Arrived at Abergavenny, nine at night, Friday, 21st.—I am now writing in my bed-room at Abergavenny, before breakfast, with the Sugar-loaf Mountain in view of my window, and before night we shall be on his brow.

I have now discovered that the hill I saw from my window is not the Sugar-loaf, but one of much inferior size. With ten in company, and three servants, it required some little order and contrivance to get us all up so rugged a way, and to such a distance. We found that as sociables and common carriages could not pass the narrow, stony, and precipitate lanes which lead up to the high ground, the best way would be to hire a carriage on purpose, that would carry half our party. We learned that a man in the neighbourhood, was in the habit of carrying strangers to the top of the Sugar-loaf, and the Skired, and Blorench, &c. and that his conveyance was a common open cart, fitted up with occasional seats for the purpose, and drawn by three little scrambling ponies. The driver and owner is a red-faced little fellow named Powel, who lives on his own small property, and is, perhaps, one of those we might call yeomen, or what in the north are termed statesmen. In this cart were stowed six of us; the rest rode single horses, chiefly fitted with side-saddles, for the accommodation of the ladies, who occasionally relieved each other. The cart was abundantly stored with provisions, wine, bottled ale, and fruit, and every thing that could render the expedition agreeable and joyous. In this style, the whole cavalcade left the Angel Inn at Abergany, and excited a great deal of mirth. The roads up the mountain are such as nothing could have passed, but a cart; brambles, honeysuckles, and hazelnuts, rapped us on the head as we jolted up the courses of the winter's torrents, for every lane is a water-course. Blorench seemed to rise in greater sublimity, as we ascended the lower hills, or base of the Sugar-loaf. Skired Vawr was on our right, but the day was hazy, and the prospect not so extensive as it sometimes is. We reached the top of the woody part of this high ground, and then had a fairer view of the peak or summit of 'Pen y Vale,' which I understand to mean the 'head of the vale,' and which somebody has since baptized by the more melting name of the 'Sugar-loaf.' I here took to my feet, and steered directly for the summit, while most of the party went slowly round with the cart; but young Parnell Cooper, rode his father's horse, amidst the rocks and fragments, almost to the summit, where the poor animal trembled and neighed for his companions. I gained the brow by regular and temperate exertion, for I had learned a lesson from Symmons' Yat, gathering whimburys or winberries in my way; and resting on the grotesque and immense fragments of rocks, which appear to have rolled down from the top; which is composed almost of entire rock, and is not a sharp, but a long narrow ridge, of about one hundred yards wide.

FROM *THE BANKS OF WYE*, BOOK III
[Invocation to the Spirit of Burns, at the summit of the Sugar-Loaf]

> Spirit of Burns! the daring child
> Of glorious freedom, rough and wild,
> How have I wept o'er all thy ills,
> How blest thy Caledonian hills!
> How almost worshipp'd in my dreams
> Thy mountain haunts,—thy classic streams!
> How burnt with hopeless, aimless fire,
> To mark thy giant strength aspire
> In patriot themes! and tun'd the while
> Thy 'Bonny Doon,' or 'Balloch Mile.'   10
> Spirit of Burns! accept the tear
> That rapture gives thy mem'ry here
> On the bleak mountain top. Here thou
> Thyself hadst rais'd the gallant brow

Of conscious intellect, to twine
Th'imperishable verse of thine,
That charms the world. Or can it be,
That scenes like these were nought to thee?
That Scottish hills so far excel,
That so deep sinks the Scottish dell,   20
That boasted Pen-y-vale had been,
For thy loud northern lyre too mean;
Broad-shoulder'd Blorenge a mere knoll,
And Skyrid, let him smile or scowl,
A dwarfish bully, vainly proud,
Because he breaks the passing cloud?
If even so, thou bard of fame,
The consequences rest the same:
For, grant that to thy infant sight
Rose mountains of stupendous height;   30
Or grant that Cambrian minstrels taught
'Mid scenes that mock the lowland thought;
Grant that old Talliesen flung
His thousand raptures, as he sung
From huge Plynlimon's awful brow,
Or Cader Idris, capt with snow;
Such Alpine scenes with them or thee
Well suited.—*These* are Alps to me.
      Long did we, noble Blorenge, gaze
On thee, and mark the eddying haze   40
That strove to reach thy level crown,
From the rich stream, and smoking town;
And oft, old Skyrid, hail'd thy name,
Nor dar'd deride thy holy fame.
Long follow'd with untiring eye
Th'illumin'd clouds, that o'er the sky
Drew their thin veil, and slowly sped,
Dipping to every mountain's head,
Dark-mingling, fading, wild, and thence,
Till admiration, in suspense,   50
Hung on the verge of sight. Then sprung,
By thousands known, by thousands sung,
Feelings that earth and time defy,
That cleave to immortality.

Song (c. 1812)

Tune.—Ligoran Cosh.

The man in the moon look'd down one night,
    Where a lad and his lass were walking;
Thinks he, there must be a very huge delight
    In this kissing and nonsense talking:
And so there must ('tis a well-known case),
    For it lasts both late and early.
For they talk'd him down, till he cover'd his face,
    —They tir'd his patience fairly.

Then up rose the sun in his morning beams,
    And push'd back his nightcap to greet them;   10
Says he,—'as you boast of your darts and flames,
    My darts and my flames shall meet them.'
He scorch'd them both through the live-long day,
    But they never seem'd to mind him,
But laugh'd outright, as he skulk'd away,
    And left a dark world behind him.

Then the man in the moon look'd down in a pet,
    And said, 'I believe I can cure you;
Though my brother has fail'd, I may conquer yet—
    If not, I must try to endure you.   20
Go home,' he cried, 'and attend to my rules,
    And banish all thoughts of sorrow;
Then jump into bed, you couple of fools,
    And you'll both be wiser to-morrow.'

Sonnet. To fifteen gnats seen dancing in the sun-beams on Jan. 3 (c. 1819)

Welcome, ye little fools, to cheer us now,
    With recollections of a summer's eve;
    And, though my heart, can not the cheat believe,
Still merrily dance about your leafless bough.
—I love you from my soul; and though I know
    Ye can *but die*—to think *how soon*, I grieve;—
Perhaps to-night the *blast of death* may blow;
    Frost be at hand—who grants you no reprieve.
—Your company's too small, I ween, that you
    Thus raise the shrill note of your summer's song;   10
Yet dance away—'tis thus that children do,—
    And wiser men to life's end dance along.
Die, little gnats, as winds or frosts ordain:—
Death is our frost too—but we fly again.

Hob's Epitaph (c. 1819)

A grey-owl was I when on earth;
    My master, a wondrous wise-man,
Found out my deserts and my worth,
    And would needs have me bred an exciseman.

He gave me the range of his house,
    And a favourite study, his shed,
Where I rush'd on the struggling mouse,
    While science rush'd into my head.

In gauging, I still made advances;
    Like schoolboy, grew wiser and wiser;   10
Resolved in the world to take chances,
    And try to come in supervisor.

But Fate comes, and Genius must fail:—
    One morning, while gauging or drinking,
My wig over-ballanced my tail,
    And I found myself stifling and sinking.

Yet I died not like men—who still quarrel
    Through life—yet to destiny yield:—
The tippler is drown'd in his barrel;
    The soldier is slain in the field.—   20

Not in love—nor in debt—nor in strife—
    Nor in horrors attendant on war:—
In a barrel I gave up my life,
    But mine was—a barrel of tar.

From May Day with the Muses (1822)

Preface

I am of opinion that Prefaces are very useless things in cases like the present, where the Author must talk of himself, with little amusement to his readers. I have hesitated whether I should say any thing or nothing; but as it is the fashion to say something, I suppose I must comply. I am well aware that many readers will exclaim—'It is not the common practice of English baronets to remit half a year's rent to their tenants for poetry, or for any thing else.' This may be very true; but I have found a character in the Rambler, No. 82, who made a very different bargain, and who says, 'And as Alfred received the tribute of the Welsh in wolves' heads, I allowed my tenants to pay their rents in butterflies, till I had exhausted the papilionaceous tribe. I then directed them to the pursuit of other animals, and obtained, by this easy method, most of the grubs and insects which land, air, or water can supply .... I have, from my own ground, the longest blade of grass upon record, and once accepted, as a half year's rent for a field of wheat, an ear, containing more grains than had been seen before upon a single stem.'

I hope my old Sir Ambrose stands in no need of defence from me or from any one; a man has a right to do what he likes with his own estate. The characters I have introduced as candidates may not come off so easily; a cluster of poets is not likely to be found in one village, and the following lines, written by my good friend T. Park, Esq. of Hampstead, are not only true, but beaufully true, and I cannot omit them.

Written in the Isle of Thanet, August, 1790

The bard, who paints from rural plains,
    Must oft himself the void supply
Of damsels pure and artless swains,
    Of innocence and industry:

For sad experience shows the heart
    Of human beings much the same;
Or polish'd by insidious art,
    Or rude as from the clod it came.

And he who roams the village round,
    Or strays amid the harvest sere,
Will hear, as now, too many a sound
    Quiet would never wish to hear.

The wrangling rustics' loud abuse,
    The coarse, unfeeling, witless jest,
The threat obscene, the oath profuse,
    And all that cultured minds detest.

Hence let those Sylvan poets glean,
    Who picture life without a flaw;
Nature may form a perfect scene,
    But Fancy must the figures draw.

The word 'fancy' connects itself with my very childhood, fifty years back.
The fancy of those who wrote the songs which I was obliged to hear in
infancy was a very inanimate and sleepy fancy. I could enumerate a dozen
songs at least which all described sleeping shepherds and shepherdesses,
and, in one instance, where they both went to sleep: this is not fair certainly;
it is not even 'watch and watch.'

As Damon and Phillis were keeping of sheep,
Being free from all care they retired to sleep, &c.

I must say, that if I understand any thing at all about keeping sheep, this
is not the way to go to work with them. But such characters and such
writings were fashionable, and fashion will beat common sense at any time.
    With all the beauty and spirit of Cunningham's 'Kate of Aberdeen,'
and some others, I never found any thing to strike my mind so forcibly
as the last stanza of Dibdin's 'Sailor's Journal'—

At length, 'twas in the month of May,
  Our crew, it being lovely weather,
At three A. M. discovered day
  And England's chalky cliffs together!
At seven, up channel how we bore,
  Whilst hopes and fears rush'd o'er each fancy!
At twelve, I gaily jump'd on shore,
  And to my throbbing heart press'd Nancy.

This, to my feelings, is a balm at all times; it is spirit, animation, and imagery, all at once.

I will plead no excuses for any thing which the reader may find in this little volume, but merely state, that I once met with a lady in London, who, though otherwise of strong mind and good information, would maintain that 'it is impossible for a blind man to fall in love.' I always thought her wrong, and the present tale of 'Alfred and Jennet' is written to elucidate my side of the question.

I have been reported to be dead; but I can assure the reader that this, like many other reports, is not true. I have written these tales in anxiety, and in a wretched state of health; and if these formidable foes have not incapacitated me, but left me free to meet the public eye with any degree of credit, that degree of credit I am sure I shall gain. I am, with remembrance of what is past,

Most respectfully,

Robert Bloomfield, Shefford, Bedfordshire, April 10th 1822.

THE INVITATION

O for the strength to paint my joy once more!
That joy I feel when Winter's reign is o'er;
When the dark despot lifts his hoary brow,
And seeks his polar-realm's eternal snow.
Though black November's fogs oppress my brain,
Shake every nerve, and struggling fancy chain;
Though time creeps o'er me with his palsied hand,
And frost-like bids the stream of passion stand,
And through his dry teeth sends a shivering blast,
And points to more than fifty winters past,   10
Why should I droop with heartless, aimless eye?
Friends start around, and all my phantoms fly,
And Hope, upsoaring with expanded wing,
Unfolds a scroll, inscribed 'Remember Spring.'
Stay, sweet enchantress, charmer of my days,
And glance thy rainbow colours o'er my lays;
Be to poor Giles what thou hast ever been,
His heart's warm solace and his sovereign queen;
Dance with his rustics when the laugh runs high,

Live in the lover's heart, the maiden's eye;   20
Still be propitious when his feet shall stray
Beneath the bursting hawthorn-buds of May;
Warm every thought, and brighten every hour,
And let him feel thy presence and thy power.
    Sir Ambrose Higham, in his eightieth year,
With memory unimpair'd, and conscience clear,
His English heart untrammell'd, and full blown
His senatorial honours and renown,
Now, basking in his plenitude of fame,
Resolved, in concert with his noble dame,   30
To drive to town no more—no more by night
To meet in crowded courts a blaze of light,
In streets a roaring mob with flags unfurl'd,
And all the senseless discord of the world,—
But calmly wait the hour of his decay,
The broad bright sunset of his glorious day;
And where he first drew breath at last to fall,
Beneath the towering shades of Oakly Hall.
    Quick spread the news through hamlet, field, and farm,
The labourer wiped his brow and staid his arm;   40
'Twas news to him of more importance far
Than change of empires or the yells of war;
It breathed a hope which nothing could destroy,
Poor widows rose, and clapp'd their hands for joy,
Glad voices rang at every cottage door,
'Good old Sir Ambrose goes to town no more.'
Well might the village bells the triumphs sound,
Well might the voice of gladness ring around;
Where sickness raged, or want allied to shame,
Sure as the sun his well-timed succour came;   50
Food for the starving child, and warmth and wine
For age that totter'd in its last decline.
From him they shared the embers' social glow;
He fed the flame that glanced along the snow,
When winter drove his storms across the sky,
And pierced the bones of shrinking poverty.
    Sir Ambrose loved the Muses, and would pay
Due honours even to the ploughman's lay;
Would cheer the feebler bard, and with the strong

Soar to the noblest energies of song;   60
Catch the rib-shaking laugh, or from his eye
Dash silently the tear of sympathy.
Happy old man!—with feelings such as these
The seasons all can charm, and trifles please;
And hence a sudden thought, a new-born whim,
Would shake his cup of pleasure to the brim,
Turn scoffs and doubts and obstacles aside,
And instant action follow like a tide.
        Time past, he had on his paternal ground
With pride the latent sparks of genius found   70
In many a local ballad, many a tale,
As wild and brief as cowslips in the dale,
Though unrecorded as the gleams of light
That vanish in the quietness of night.
'Why not,' he cried, as from his couch he rose,
'To cheer my age, and sweeten my repose,
Why not be just and generous in time,
And bid my tenants pay their rents in rhyme?
For one half year they shall.—A feast shall bring
A crowd of merry faces in the spring;—   80
Here, pens, boy, pens; I'll weigh the case no more,
But write the summons:—go, go, shut the door.
    "All ye on Oakly manor dwelling,
      Farming, labouring, buying, selling,
      Neighbours! banish gloomy looks,
      My grey old steward shuts his books.
      Let not a thought of winter's rent
      Destroy one evening's merriment;
      I ask not gold, but tribute found
      Abundant on Parnassian ground.   90
      Choose, ye who boast the gift, your themes
      Of joy or pathos, tales or dreams,
      Choose each a theme;—but, harkye, bring
      No stupid ghost, no vulgar thing;
      Fairies, indeed, may wind their way,
      And sparkle through the brightest lay:
      I love their pranks, their favourite green,
      And, could the little sprites be seen,
      Were I a king, I'd sport with them,

And dance beneath my diadem.   100
But surely fancy need not brood
O'er midnight darkness, crimes, and blood,
In magic cave or monk's retreat,
Whilst the bright world is at her feet;
Whilst to her boundless range is given,
By night, by day, the lights of heaven,
And all they shine upon; whilst Love
Still reigns the monarch of the grove,
And real life before her lies
In all its thousand, thousand dies.   110
Then bring me nature, bring me sense,
And joy shall be your recompense:
On Old May-day I hope to see
All happy: leave the rest to me.
A general feast shall cheer us all
Upon the lawn that fronts the hall,
With tents for shelter, laurel boughs,
And wreaths of every flower that blows.
The months are wending fast away;
Farewell, remember Old May-day.'"   120
Surprise, and mirth, and gratitude, and jeers,
The clown's broad wonder, th'enthusiast's tears,
Fresh gleams of comfort on the brow of care,
The sectary's cold shrug, the miser's stare,
Were all excited, for the tidings flew
As quick as scandal the whole country through.
'Rent paid by rhymes at Oakly may be great,
But rhymes for taxes would appal the state,'
Exclaim'd th'exciseman,—'and then tithes, alas!
Why there, again, 'twill never come to pass.'—   130
Thus all still ventured, as the whim inclined,
Remarks as various as the varying mind:
For here Sir Ambrose sent a challenge forth,
That claim'd a tribute due to sterling worth;
And all, whatever might their host regale,
Agreed to share the feast and drink his ale.
     Now shot through many a heart a secret fire,
A new born spirit, an intense desire
For once to catch a spark of local fame,

And bear a poet's honourable name! 140
Already some aloft began to soar,
And some to think who never thought before;
But O, what numbers all their strength applied,
Then threw despairingly the task aside
With feign'd contempt, and vow'd they'd never tried.
Did dairy-wife neglect to turn her cheese,
Or idling miller lose the favouring breeze;
Did the young ploughman o'er the furrows stand,
Or stalking sower swing an empty hand,
One common sentence on their heads would fall, 150
'Twas Oakly banquet had bewitch'd them all.
Loud roar'd the winds of March, with whirling snow,
One brightening hour an April breeze would blow;
Now hail, now hoar-frost bent the flow'ret's head,
Now struggling beams their languid influence shed,
That scarce a cowering bird yet dared to sing
'Midst the wild changes of our island spring.
Yet, shall the Italian goatherd boasting cry,
'Poor Albion! when hadst thou so clear a sky!'
And deem that nature smiles for him alone; 160
Her renovated beauties all his own?
No:—let our April showers by night descend,
Noon's genial warmth with twilight stillness blend;
The broad Atlantic pour her pregnant breath,
And rouse the vegetable world from death;
Our island spring is rapture's self to me,
All I have seen, and all I wish to see.
      Thus came the jovial day, no streaks of red
O'er the broad portal of the morn were spread,
But one high-sailing mist of dazzling white, 170
A screen of gossamer, a magic light,
Doom'd instantly, by simplest shepherd's ken,
To reign awhile, and be exhaled at ten.
O'er leaves, o'er blossoms, by his power restored,
Forth came the conquering sun and look'd abroad;
Millions of dew-drops fell, yet millions hung,
Like words of transport trembling on the tongue
Too strong for utt'rance:—Thus the infant boy,
With rosebud cheeks, and features tuned to joy,

Weeps while he struggles with restraint or pain,   180
But change the scene, and make him laugh again,
His heart rekindles, and his cheek appears
A thousand times more lovely through his tears.
From the first glimpse of day a busy scene
Was that high swelling lawn, that destined green,
Which shadowless expanded far and wide,
The mansion's ornament, the hamlet's pride;
To cheer, to order, to direct, contrive,
Even old Sir Ambrose had been up at five;
There his whole household labour'd in his view,—   190
But light is labour where the task is new.
Some wheel'd the turf to build a grassy throne
Round a huge thorn that spread his boughs alone,
Rough-rined and bold, as master of the place;
Five generations of the Higham race
Had pluck'd his flowers, and still he held his sway,
Waved his white head, and felt the breath of May.
Some from the green-house ranged exotics round,
To bask in open day on English ground:
And 'midst them in a line of splendour drew   200
Long wreaths and garlands, gather'd in the dew.
Some spread the snowy canvas, propp'd on high
O'er shelter'd tables with their whole supply;
Some swung the biting scythe with merry face,
And cropp'd the daisies for a dancing space.
Some roll'd the mouldy barrel in his might,
From prison'd darkness into cheerful light,
And fenced him round with cans; and others bore
The creaking hamper with its costly store,
Well cork'd, well flavour'd, and well tax'd, that came   210
From Lusitanian mountains, dear to fame,
Whence Gama steer'd, and led the conquering way
To eastern triumphs and the realms of day.
A thousand minor tasks fill'd every hour,
'Till the sun gain'd the zenith of his power,
When every path was throng'd with old and young,
And many a sky-lark in his strength upsprung
To bid them welcome.—Not a face was there
But for May-day at least had banish'd care;

No cringing looks, no pauper tales to tell,   220
No timid glance, they knew their host too well,—
Freedom was there, and joy in every eye:
Such scenes were England's boast in days gone by.
Beneath the thorn was good Sir Ambrose found,
His guests an ample crescent form'd around;
Nature's own carpet spread the space between,
Where blithe domestics plied in gold and green.
The venerable chaplain waved his wand,
And silence follow'd as he stretch'd his hand,
And with a trembling voice, and heart sincere,   230
Implored a blessing on th'abundant cheer.
Down sat the mingling throng, and shared a feast
With hearty welcomes given, by love increased;
A patriarch family, a close-link'd band,
True to their rural chieftain, heart and hand:
The deep carouse can never boast the bliss,
The animation of a scene like this.
       At length the damask cloths were whisk'd away,
Like fluttering sails upon a summer's day;
The hey-day of enjoyment found repose;   240
The worthy baronet majestic rose;
They view'd him, while his ale was filling round,
The monarch of his own paternal ground.
His cup was full, and where the blossoms bow'd
Over his head, Sir Ambrose spoke aloud,
Nor stopp'd a dainty form or phrase to cull—
His heart elated, like his cup, was full:—
'Full be your hopes, and rich the crops that fall;
Health to my neighbours, happiness to all.'
Dull must that clown be, dull as winter's sleet,   250
Who would not instantly be on his feet:
An echoing health to mingling shouts gave place,
'Sir Ambrose Higham, and his noble race.'
       Avaunt, Formality! thou bloodless dame,
With dripping besom quenching nature's flame;
Thou cankerworm, who liv'st but to destroy,
And eat the very heart of social joy;—
Thou freezing mist round intellectual mirth,
Thou spell-bound vagabond of spurious birth,

Away! away! and let the sun shine clear,   260
And all the kindnesses of life appear.
    With mild complacency, and smiling brow,
The host look'd round, and bade the goblets flow;
Yet curiously anxious to behold
Who first would pay in rhymes instead of gold;
Each eye inquiring through the ring was glanced
To see who dared the task, who first advanced;
That instant started Philip from the throng,
Philip, a farmer's son, well known for song,—
And, as the mingling whispers round him ran,   270
He humbly bow'd, and timidly began:—

THE DRUNKEN FATHER

Poor Ellen married Andrew Hall,
    Who dwells beside the moor,
Where yonder rose-tree shades the wall,
    And woodbines grace the door.

Who does not know how blest, how loved
    Were her mild laughing eyes
By every youth!—but Andrew proved
    Unworthy of his prize.

In tippling was his whole delight,   280
    Each sign-post barr'd his way;
He spent in muddy ale at night
    The wages of the day.

Though Ellen still had charms, was young,
    And he in manhood's prime,
She sad beside her cradle sung,
    And sigh'd away her time.

One cold bleak night, the stars were hid,
    In vain she wish'd him home;
Her children cried, half cheer'd, half chid,   290
    'O when will father come!'

'Till Caleb, nine years old, upsprung,
 And kick'd his stool aside,
And younger Mary round him clung,
 'I'll go, and you shall guide.'

The children knew each inch of ground,
 Yet Ellen had her fears;
Light from the lantern glimmer'd round,
 And show'd her falling tears.

'Go by the mill and down the lane;   300
 Return the same way home:
Perhaps you'll meet him, give him light;
 O how I *wish* he'd come!'

Away they went, as close and true
 As lovers in the shade,
And Caleb swung his father's staff
 At every step he made.

The noisy mill-clack rattled on,
 They saw the water flow,
And leap in silvery foam along,   310
 Deep murmuring below.

'We'll soon be there,' the hero said,
 'Come on, 'tis but a mile,—
Here's where the cricket-match was play'd,
 And here's the shady stile.

How the light shines up every bough!
 How strange the leaves appear!
Hark!—What was that?—'tis silent now,
 Come, Mary, never fear.'

The staring oxen breathed aloud,   320
 But never dream'd of harm;
A meteor glanced along the cloud
 That hung o'er Wood-Hill Farm.

Old Caesar bark'd and howl'd hard by,
    All else was still as death,
But Caleb was ashamed to cry,
    And Mary held her breath.

At length they spied a distant light,
    And heard a chorus brawl;
Wherever drunkards stopp'd at night,   330
    Why there was Andrew Hall.

The house was full, the landlord gay,
    The bar-maid shook her head,
And wish'd the boobies far away
    That kept her out of bed.

There Caleb enter'd, firm, but mild,
    And spoke in plaintive tone:—
'My mother could not leave the child,
    So we are come alone.'

E'en drunken Andrew felt the blow   340
    That innocence can give,
When its resistless accents flow
    To bid affection live.

'I'm coming, loves, I'm coming now,'—
    Then, shuffling o'er the floor,
Contrived to make his balance true,
    And led them from the door.

The plain broad path that brought him there
    By day, though faultless then,
Was up and down and narrow grown,   350
    Though wide enough for ten.

The stiles were wretchedly contrived,
    The stars were all at play,
And many a ditch had moved itself
    Exactly in his way.

Onward he stepp'd, the boy alert,
    Calling his courage forth,
Hung like a log on Andrew's skirt,   390
    And down he brought them both.

The tumb'ling lantern reach'd the stream,
    Its hissing light soon gone;
'Twas night, without a single gleam,
    And terror reign'd alone.

A general scream the miller heard,
    Then rubb'd his eyes and ran,
And soon his welcome light appear'd,
    As grumbling he began:—

'What have we here, and whereabouts?   400
    Why what a hideous squall!
Some drunken fool! I thought as much—
    'Tis only Andrew Hall!

Poor children!' tenderly he said,
    'But now the danger's past.'
They thank'd him for his light and aid,
    And drew near home at last.

But who upon the misty path
    To meet them forward press'd?
'Twas Ellen, shivering, with a babe   410
    Close folded to her breast.

Said Andrew, 'Now you're glad, I know,
    To se-se-see us come;—
But I have taken care of both,
    And brought them bo-bo-both safe home.'

With Andrew vex'd, of Mary proud,
    But prouder of her boy,
She kiss'd them both, and sobb'd aloud,—
    The children cried for joy.

But what a home at last they found!   420
    Of comforts all bereft;
The fire out, the last candle gone,
    And not one penny left!

But Caleb quick as lightning flew,
    And raised a light instead;
And as the kindling brands he blew,
    His father snored in bed.

No brawling, boxing termagant
    Was Ellen, though offended;
Who ever knew a fault like this   430
    By violence amended?

No:—she was mild as April morn,
    And Andrew loved her too;
She rose at daybreak, though forlorn,
    To try what love could do.

And as her waking husband groan'd,
    And roll'd his burning head,
She spoke with all the power of truth,
    Down kneeling by his bed.

'Dear Andrew, hear me,—though distress'd   440
    Almost too much to speak,—
This infant starves upon my breast—
    To scold I am too weak.

I work, I spin, I toil all day,
    Then leave my work to cry,
And start with horror when I think
    You wish to see me die.

But *do* you wish it? can that bring
    More comfort, or more joy?
Look round the house, how destitute!   450
    Look at your ragged boy!

That boy should make a father proud,
    If any feeling can;
Then save your children, save your wife,
    Your honour as a man.

Hear me, for God's sake hear me now,
    And act a father's part!'
The culprit bless'd her angel tongue,
    And clasp'd her to his heart;

And would have vow'd, and would have sworn,   460
    But Ellen kiss'd him dumb,—
'Exert your mind, vow *to yourself,*
    And better days will come.

I shall be well when you are kind,
    And you'll be better too.'—
'I'll drink no more,'—he quick rejoin'd,—
    'Be't poison if I do.'

From that bright day his plants, his flowers,
    His crops began to thrive,
And for three years has Andrew been   470
    The soberest man alive.

Soon as he ended, acclamations 'rose,
Endang'ring modesty and self-repose,
Till the good host his prudent counsel gave,
Then listen'd all, the flippant and the grave.
'Let not applauses vanity inspire,
Deter humility, or damp desire;
Neighbours we are, then let the stream run fair,
And every couplet be as free as air;
Be silent when each speaker claims his right,   480
Enjoy the day as I enjoy the sight:
They shall not class us with the knavish elves,
Who banish shame, and criticise themselves.'
    Thenceforward converse flow'd with perfect ease,
Midst country wit, and rustic repartees.

One drank to Ellen, if such might be found,
And archly glanced at female faces round.
If one with tilted can began to bawl,
Another cried, 'Remember Andrew Hall.'
Then, multifarious topics, corn and hay,   490
Vestry intrigues, the rates they had to pay,
The thriving stock, the lands too wet, too dry,
And all that bears on fruitful husbandry,
Ran mingling through the crowd—a crowd that might,
Transferr'd to canvas, give the world delight;
A scene that Wilkie might have touch'd with pride—
The May-day banquet then had never died.
    But who is he, uprisen, with eye so keen,
In garb of shining plush of grassy green—
Dogs climbing round him, eager for the start,   500
With ceaseless tail, and doubly beating heart?
A stranger, who from distant forests came,
The sturdy keeper of the Oakly game.
Short prelude made, he pointed o'er the hill,
And raised a voice that every ear might fill;
His heart was in his theme, and in the forest still.

    THE FORESTER

Born in a dark wood's lonely dell,
    Where echoes roar'd, and tendrils curl'd
Round a low cot, like hermit's cell,
    Old Salcey Forest was my world.   510
I felt no bonds, no shackles then,
    For life in freedom was begun;
I gloried in th'exploits of men,
    And learn'd to lift my father's gun.

O what a joy it gave my heart!
    Wild as a woodbine up I grew;
Soon in his feats I bore a part,
    And counted all the game he slew.
I learn'd the wiles, the shifts, the calls,
    The language of each living thing;   520
I mark'd the hawk that darting falls,
    Or station'd spreads the trembling wing.

I mark'd the owl that silent flits,
    The hare that feeds at eventide,
The upright rabbit, when he sits
    And mocks you, ere he deigns to hide.
I heard the fox bark through the night,
    I saw the rooks depart at morn,
I saw the wild deer dancing light,
    And heard the hunter's cheering horn.   530

Mad with delight, I roam'd around
    From morn to eve throughout the year,
But still, midst all I sought or found,
    My favourites were the spotted deer.
The elegant, the branching brow,
    The doe's clean limbs and eyes of love;
The fawn as white as mountain snow,
    That glanced through fern and brier and grove.

One dark, autumnal, stormy day,
    The gale was up in all its might,   540
The roaring forest felt its sway,
    And clouds were scudding quick as light:
A ruthless crash, a hollow groan,
    Aroused each self-preserving start,
The kine in herds, the hare alone,
    And shagged colts that grazed apart.

Midst fears instinctive, wonder drew
    The boldest forward, gathering strength
As darkness lour'd, and whirlwinds blew,
    To where the ruin stretch'd his length.   550
The shadowing oak, the noblest stem
    That graced the forest's ample bound,
Had cast to earth his diadem;
    His fractured limbs had delved the ground.

He lay, and still to fancy groan'd;
    He lay like Alfred when he died—
Alfred, a king by Heaven enthroned,
    His age's wonder, England's pride!

Monarch of forests, great as good,
    Wise as the sage,—thou heart of steel!   560
Thy name shall rouse the patriot's blood
    As long as England's sons can feel.

From every lawn, and copse, and glade,
    The timid deer in squadrons came,
And circled round their fallen shade
    With all of language but its name.
Astonishment and dread withheld
    The fawn and doe of tender years,
But soon a triple circle swell'd,
    With rattling horns and twinkling ears.   570

Some in his root's deep cavern housed,
    And seem'd to learn, and muse, and teach,
Or on his topmost foliage browsed,
    That had for centuries mock'd their reach.
Winds in their wrath these limbs could crash,
    This strength, this symmetry could mar;
A people's wrath can monarchs dash
    From bigot throne or purple car.

When Fate's dread bolt in Clermont's bowers
    Provoked its million tears and sighs,   580
A nation wept its fallen flowers,
    Its blighted hopes, its darling prize.—
So mourn'd my antler'd friends awhile,
    So dark, so dread, the fateful day;
So mourn'd the herd that knew no guile,
    Then turn'd disconsolate away!

Who then of language will be proud?
    Who arrogate that gift of heaven?
To wild herds when they bellow loud,
    To all the forest-tribes 'tis given.   590
I've heard a note from dale or hill
    That lifted every head and eye;
I've heard a scream aloft, so shrill
    That terror seized on all that fly.

Empires may fall, and nations groan,
    Pride be thrown down, and power decay;
Dark bigotry may rear her throne,
    But science is the light of day.
Yet, while so low my lot is cast,
    Through wilds and forests let me range;   600
My joys shall pomp and power outlast—
    The voice of nature cannot change.

A soberer feeling through the crowd he flung,
Clermont was uppermost on every tongue;
But who can live on unavailing sighs?
The inconsolable are not the wise.
Spirit, and youth, and worth, demand a tear—
That day was past, and sorrow was not here;
Sorrow the contest dared not but refuse
'Gainst Oakly's open cellar and the muse.   610
    Sir Ambrose cast his eye along the line,
Where many a cheerful face began to shine,
And, fixing on his man, cried, loud and clear,
'What have you brought, John Armstrong? let us hear.'
Forth stepp'd his shepherd;—scanty locks of grey—
Edged round a hat that seem'd to mock decay;
Its loops, its bands, were from the purest fleece,
Spun on the hills in silence and in peace.
A staff he bore carved round with birds and flowers,
The hieroglyphics of his leisure hours;   620
And rough-form'd animals of various name,
Not just like Bewick's, but they meant the same.
Nor these alone his whole attention drew,
He was a poet,—this Sir Ambrose knew,—
A strange one too;—and now had penn'd a lay,
Harmless and wild, and fitting for the day.
No tragic tale on stilts;—his mind had more
Of boundless frolic than of serious lore;—
Down went his hat, his shaggy friend close by
Dozed on the grass, yet watch'd his master's eye.   630

THE SHEPHERD'S DREAM: OR, FAIRIES' MASQUERADE

I had folded my flock, and my heart was o'erflowing,
I loiter'd beside the small lake on the heath;
The red sun, though down, left his drapery glowing,
And no sound was stirring, I heard not a breath:
I sat on the turf, but I meant not to sleep,
And gazed o'er that lake which for ever is new,
Where clouds over clouds appear'd anxious to peep
From this bright double sky with its pearl and its blue.

Forgetfulness, rather than slumber, it seem'd,
When in infinite thousands the fairies arose   640
All over the heath, and their tiny crests gleam'd
In mock'ry of soldiers, our friends and our foes.
There a stripling went forth, half a finger's length high,
And led a huge host to the north with a dash;
Silver birds upon poles went before their wild cry,
While the monarch look'd forward, adjusting his sash.

Soon after a terrible bonfire was seen,
The dwellings of fairies went down in their ire,
But from all I remember, I never could glean
Why the woodstack was burnt, or who set it on fire.   650
The flames seem'd to rise o'er a deluge of snow,
That buried its thousands,—the rest ran away;
For the hero had here overstrain'd his long bow,
Yet he honestly own'd the mishap of the day.

Then the fays of the north like a hailstorm came on,
And follow'd him down to the lake in a riot,
Where they found a large stone which they fix'd him upon,
And threaten'd, and coax'd him, and bade him be quiet.
He that conquer'd them all, was to conquer no more,
But the million beheld he could conquer alone;   660
After resting awhile, he leap'd boldly on shore,
When away ran a fay that had mounted his throne.

'Twas pleasant to see how they stared, how they scamper'd,
By furze-bush, by fern, by no obstacle stay'd,
And the few that held council, were terribly hamper'd,
For some were vindictive, and some were afraid.

I saw they were dress'd for a masquerade train,
Colour'd rags upon sticks they all brandish'd in view,
And of such idle things they seem'd mightily vain,
Though they nothing display'd but a bird split in two.   670

Then out rush'd the stripling in battle array,
And both sides determined to fight and to maul:
Death rattled his jawbones to see such a fray,
And glory personified laugh'd at them all.
Here he fail'd,—hence he fled, with a few for his sake,
And leap'd into a cockle-shell floating hard by;
It sail'd to an isle in the midst of the lake,
Where they mock'd fallen greatness, and left him to die.

Meanwhile the north fairies stood round in a ring,
Supporting his rival on guns and on spears,   680
Who, though not a soldier, was robed like a king;
Yet some were exulting, and some were in tears.
A lily triumphantly floated above,
The crowd press'd, and wrangling was heard through the whole;
Some soldiers look'd surly, some citizens strove
To hoist the old nightcap on liberty's pole.

But methought in my dream some bewail'd him that fell,
And liked not his victors so gallant, so clever,
Till a fairy stepp'd forward, and blew through a shell,
'Bear misfortune with firmness, you'll triumph for ever.'   690
I woke at the sound, all in silence, alone,
The moor-hens were floating like specks on a glass,
The dun clouds were spreading, the vision was gone,
And my dog scamper'd round 'midst the dew on the grass.

I took up my staff, as a knight would his lance,
And said, 'Here's my sceptre, my baton, my spear,
And there's my prime minister far in advance,
Who serves me with truth for his food by the year.'
So I slept without care till the dawning of day,
Then trimm'd up my woodbines and whistled amain;   700
My minister heard as he bounded away,
And we led forth our sheep to their pastures again.

[THE END OF THE COMPETITION]

Here rest thee, rest thee, Muse, review the scene
Where thou with me from peep of dawn hast been:
We did not promise that this motley throng
Should every *one* supply a votive song,
Nor every tenant:—yet thou hast been kind,
For untold tales must still remain behind,
Which might o'er listening patience still prevail,
Did fancy waver not, nor daylight fail.
'The Soldier's Wife,' her toils, his battles o'er,
'Love in a Shower,' the riv'let's sudden roar;   10
Then, 'Lines to Aggravation' form the close,
Parent of murders, and the worst of woes.
But while the changeful hours of daylight flew,
Some homeward look'd, and talk'd of evening dew;
Some watch'd the sun's decline, and stroll'd around,
Some wish'd another dance, and partners found;
When in an instant every eye was drawn
To one bright object on the upper lawn;
A fair procession from the mansion came,
Unknown its purport, and unknown its aim.   20
No gazer could refrain, no tongue could cease,
It seem'd an embassy of love and peace.
Nearer and nearer still approach'd the train,
Age in the van transform'd to youth again.
Sir Ambrose gazed, and scarce believed his eyes;
'Twas magic, memory, love, and blank surprise,
For there his venerable lady wore
The very dress which, sixty years before,
Had sparkled on her sunshine bridal morn,
Had sparkled, ay, beneath this very thorn!   30
Her hair was snowy white, o'er which was seen,
Emblem of what her bridal cheeks had been,
A twin red rose—no other ornament
Had pride suggested, or false feeling lent;
She came to grace the triumph of her lord,
And pay him honours at his festive board.
Nine ruddy lasses follow'd where she stepp'd;
White were their virgin robes, that lightly swept

The downy grass; in every laughing eye
Cupid had skulk'd, and written 'victory.'   40
What heart on earth its homage could refuse?
Each tripp'd, unconsciously, a blushing Muse.
A slender chaplet of fresh blossoms bound
Their clustering ringlets in a magic round.
And, as they slowly moved across the green,
Each in her beauty seem'd a May-day queen.
The first a wreath bore in her outstretch'd hand,
The rest a single rose upon a wand;
Their steps were measured to that grassy throne
Where, watching them, Sir Ambrose sat alone.   50
They stopp'd,—when she, the foremost of the row,
Curtsied, and placed the wreath upon his brow;
The rest, in order pacing by his bower,
In the loop'd wreath left each her single flower,—
Then stood aside.—What broke the scene's repose?
The whole assembly clapp'd their hands and rose.
The Muses charm'd them as they form'd a ring,
And look'd the very life and soul of Spring!
But still the white hair'd dame they view'd with pride,
Her love so perfect, and her truth so tried.   60
Oh, sweet it is to hear, to see, to name,
Unquench'd affection in the palsied frame—
To think upon the boundless raptures past,
And love, triumphant, conquering to the last!
    Silenced by feeling, vanquish'd by his tears,
The host sprung up, nor felt the weight of years;
Yet utterance found not, though in virtue's cause,
But acclamations fill'd up nature's pause,
Till, by one last and vigorous essay,
His tide of feeling roll'd itself away;   70
The language of delight its bondage broke,
And many a warm heart bless'd him as he spoke.
    'Neighbours and friends, by long experience proved,
Pardon this weakness; I was too much moved:
My dame, you see, can youth and age insnare,
In vain I strove, 'twas more than I could bear,—
Yet hear me,—though the tyrant passions strive,
The words of truth, like leading stars, survive;

I thank you all, but will accomplish more,—
Your verses shall not die as heretofore;   80
Your local tales shall not be thrown away,
Nor war remain the theme of every lay.
Ours is an humbler task, that may release
The high-wrought soul, and mould it into peace.
These pastoral notes some victor's ear may fill,
Breathed amidst blossoms, where the drum is still:
I purpose then to send them forth to try
The public patience, or its apathy.
The world shall see them; why should I refrain?
'Tis all the produce of my own domain.   90
Farewell!' he said, then took his lady's arm,
On his shrunk hand her starting tears fell warm;
Again he turn'd to view the happy crowd,
And cried, 'Good night, good night, good night,' aloud,
'Health to you all! for see, the evening closes,'
Then march'd to rest, beneath his crown of roses.
'Happy old man! with feelings such as these,
The seasons all can charm, and trifles please.'
An instantaneous shout re-echoed round,
'Twas wine and gratitude inspired the sound: 100
Some joyous souls resumed the dance again,
The aged loiter'd o'er the homeward plain,
And scatter'd lovers rambled through the park,
And breathed their vows of honour in the dark;
Others a festal harmony preferr'd,
Still round the thorn the jovial song was heard;
Dance, rhymes, and fame, they scorn'd such things as these,
But drain'd the mouldy barrel to its lees,
As if 'twere worse than shame to want repose:
Nor was the lawn clear till the moon arose,   110
And on each turret pour'd a brilliant gleam
Of modest light, that trembled on the stream;
The owl awoke, but dared not yet complain,
And banish'd silence re-assumed her reign.

Songs from *Hazelwood Hall* (1823)

GLEE FOR THREE VOICES

Love in a show'r safe shelter took
In a rosy bow'r beside a brook,
And wink'd and nodded, with conscious pride
To his votaries, drench'd on the other side;
'Come hither, sweet maids, there's a bridge below,
The toll-keeper, Hymen, will let you through—
      Come over the stream to me.'

Then over they went in a huddle together,
Not caring much about wind or weather;
The bow'r was sweet, and the show'r was gone,   10
Again broke forth th'enlivening sun;
Some wish'd to return, but the toll-keeper said,
'You're a wife now, lassy, I pass'd you a maid;
      Get back as you can for me!'

SIMPLE PLEASURES

Thus thinks the trav'ler, journeying still,
    Where mountains rise sublime;
What but these scenes the heart can fill,
What charm like yonder giant hill?
    —A molehill clothed with thyme.

What can exceed the joy of pow'r?
    —That joy which conquerors prove
In sceptred rule—where all must cow'r;
What can exceed that mad'ning hour?
    —Why, peace—and home—and love!   10

From *The Bird and Insect's Post Office* (1824)

LETTER V. FROM AN EARWIG
DEPLORING THE LOSS OF ALL HER CHILDREN

Dear Aunt,

you cannot think how distressed I have been, and still am; for, under the bark of a large elm, which, I dare say, has stood there a great while, I had placed my whole family, where they were dry, comfortable, and, as I foolishly thought, secure. But only mark what calamities may fall upon earwigs before they are aware of them! I had just got my family about me, all white, clean, and promising children; when pounce came down that bird they call a woodpecker; when, thrusting his huge beak under the bark where they lay, down went our whole sheltering roof! and my children, poor things, running, as they thought, from danger, were devoured as fast as the destroyer could open his beak and shut it. For my own part, I crept into a crack in the solid tree, where I have this far escaped; but as this bird can make large holes into solid timber, I am by no means safe.

This calamity is the more heavy, as it carries with it a great disappointment: for very near our habitation was a high wall, the sunny side of which was covered with the most delicious fruits; peaches, apricots, nectarines, &c. all just then ripening; and I thought of having such a feast with my children as I had never enjoyed in my life.

I am surrounded by wood-peckers, jack-daws, magpies, and other devouring creatures, and think myself very unfortunate. Yet, perhaps, if I could know the situation of some larger creatures—I mean particularly such as would tread me to death if I crossed their path—they may have complaints to make as well as I.

Take care of yourself, my good old aunt, and I shall keep in my hiding-place as long as starvation will permit. And, after all, perhaps the fruit was not so delicious as it looked—I am resolved to think so, just to comfort myself.

Yours, with compliments, as usual.

[THE AUTHOR'S EPITAPH]

First made a Farmer's Boy, and then a snob,
A poet he became, and here lies Bob.
April 1823

But still conceit was uppermost,
    That stupid kind of pride:—
'Dost think I cannot see a post?
    Dost think I want a guide?

Why, Mary, how you twist and twirl!   360
    Why dost not keep the track?
I'll carry thee home safe, my girl,'—
    Then swung her on his back.

Poor Caleb muster'd all his wits
    To bear the light ahead,
As Andrew reel'd and stopp'd by fits,
    Or ran with thund'ring tread.

Exult, ye brutes, traduc'd and scorn'd,
    Though true to nature's plan;
Exult, ye bristled, and ye horn'd,   370
    When infants govern man.

Down to the mill-pool's dangerous brink
    The headlong party drove;
The boy alone had power to think,
    While Mary scream'd above.

'Stop!' Caleb cried, 'you've lost the path;
    The water's close before;
I see it shine, 'tis very deep,—
    Why, don't you hear it roar?'

And then in agony exclaim'd,   380
    'O where's my mother *now*?'
The Solomon of hops and malt
    Stopp'd short and made a bow:

His head was loose, his neck disjointed,
    It cost him little trouble;
But, to be stopp'd and disappointed,
    Poh! danger was a bubble.

NOTES

Notes from early editions which appear to be by Bloomfield himself are marked 'RB'.

The Farmer's Boy Text: *Poems* (1809).

SPRING. I

37   *Grafton* Augustus Henry Fitzroy, third duke of Grafton (1735-1811), Bloomfield's patron.

38   *Euston* Euston Hall, near Thetford, West Suffolk, seat of the dukes of Grafton (and the setting for 'The Fakenham Ghost'). See Brayley, *Views in Suffolk*, 1806, pp. 27-9.

223   *Gibeonite* A slave. The inhabitants of Gibeon were condemned by Joshua to be hewers of wood and drawers of water (*Joshua*, 9: 21).

250   *Orwell...Waveny...Ouse* Rivers in East Anglia.

254   *'three times skimm'd sky-blue'* Thin, watery milk which has been thoroughly skimmed and so has a bluish tinge to it.

AUTUMN. III

91   *new-briar'd* Possibly as a protection against body-snatchers.

110   *lovely Ann* 'In the description of the Mad Girl I had originally called her *Poll*; but on my visit to Suffolk, after an absence of twelve years... I learned that her name was *Ann*. I conversed with her, and found her greatly recovered, and sensible of her past calamity' (RB, in *Poems*, 1809, I, p. xxxvii). See also Brayley, *Views in Suffolk*, p. 36.

238   *Howard* John Howard (1726?-1790), philanthropist and prison reformer. Compare Thomson's praise of a 'generous band' of earlier prison reformers in *The Seasons* (1726-30; 'Winter', ll. 359-61).

260   *Euston...Fitzroy* See notes to 'Spring', ll. 37-8, above.

288   *view-halloo* A shout given by a huntsman on seeing a fox break cover.

332   *'Foxes rejoice! here buried lies your foe!'* 'Inscribed on a stone in Euston Park wall' (RB).

WINTER. IV

37   *beetle* 'An implement consisting of a heavy weight or "head," usually of wood, with a handle or stock, used for driving wedges or pegs, ramming down paving stones, or for crushing, bruising, beating, flattening or smoothing, in various industrial and domestic operations, and having various shapes according to the purpose for which it is used' (*OED*, 'beetle', 1).

153-212 Compare John Clare's two poems, 'The Death of Dobbin' and 'Death of Dobbin', *Early Poems*, ed. Eric Robinson, David Powell, and P.M.S. Dawson (Oxford, 1989), I, p. 84 and II, p. 630.

334 *teeming Ewes* Pregnant sheep; one of several phrases borrowed from John Dyer, *The Fleece* (1757), I, l. 489, the main literary source for shepherding description in the poem.

Rural Tales Text: *Poems* (1809), except for the Preface from *Rural Tales* (1802).

RICHARD AND KATE

2   *orts* Leftovers, usually of food, but here probably meaning remnants of wool from Kate's spinning.

29-30 *Wall...Band...Lucks...Twitches* 'Terms used in spinning' (1802). 'Wall' is presumably a variant of 'whorl', the weight on a spindle which acts as the pulley when it is mounted to a spinning-wheel. The 'band' is the driving belt between the wheel and the spindle. 'Lucks' are small portions of wool, twisted on the finger of the spinner of the distaff. 'Twitches' are pieces of wood wound round the forefinger of the left hand from which yarn is spun. See Eliza Leadbetter, *Spinning and Spinning Wheels* (Princes Risborough, Aylesbury: Shire Publications, 1979), pp. 3-4; Joseph Wright, *The English Dialect Dictionary* (London: Henry Frowde, 1898-1905), III, p. 683 and VI, p. 289.

31   *Hutch* 'a chest' (RB).

45   *Mawther* A girl.

50   *Gotch* 'a pitcher' (RB).

83   *Dicky Races* Donkey races.

92   *High-lows* Boots which cover the ankles.

94   *kedge* Brisk, lively, in good spirits.

WINTER SONG

12   *We'll make him at home to a pin* A pin is a small cask or keg holding half a firkin (four and a half gallons), offering the possible meaning of 'We shall acquaint him [make him feel 'at home'] with a good drink.' There are also several phrases of obscure origin associating the word 'pin' with merriness, e.g. 'upon a jolly pin'. See *OED*, 'pin,' sb. 1, 15.

Good Tidings; or, News from the Farm Text: *Poems* (1809). Bloomfield's original title for the poem was 'The Vaccine Rose'.

[II. The discovery of inoculation and vaccination]

5   *Montagu* Lady Mary Wortley Montagu (1689-1762), poet and writer. In 1716 she travelled with her husband to Constantinople, where she saw inoculation practiced. A survivor of smallpox herself, she became on her return an energetic campaigner for inoculation, winning many supporters including members of the royal family, and defying intense hostility from some quarters. See *The Turkish Embassy Letters*, ed. Malcolm Jack (London: Virago, 1993); R. Halsband, *The Life of Lady Mary Wortley Montagu* (London: Oxford University Press, 1956).

12 *by the Severn side* Edward Jenner's first work on inoculation was carried out at his practice in Berkeley, Gloucestershire, near the river Severn, used by poets to evoke the 'georgic' values associated with the border region of 'Siluria' through which it flows. Cf. 'Spring,' l. 264. See John Barrell, *The Dark Side of the Landscape* (1980), p. 173n; John Goodridge, *Rural Life in Eighteenth-Century English Poetry* (1995), pp. 178-9, both Cambridge: Cambridge University Press.

[III. Smallpox is brought into the poet's home]

11 *life's silent sand* Cf. 'The Widow to Her Hour-glass,' l. 11, 'streaming sand'.

13 *interdicted* Forbidden.

'Song sung by Mr Bloomfield' Text: *Remains* (1824), I, pp. 49-50.

'To His Wife' Text: *Remains* (1824), I, pp. 18-19.

'To a Spindle' Text: *Remains* (1824), I, pp. 20-3. A 'paralytic affection' (see the prose introduction) is what we would now call a 'stroke'.

Wild Flowers Text: *Poems* (1809), except for the Preface from *Wild Flowers* (1806). Bloomfield replaced the latter in the 1809 edition with the following short 'Advertisement': 'To continue the former Preface in this volume of "Wild Flowers" would be unnecessary: but the Dedication, because it cannot give offence, or disgust the reader, may be worthy of preservation.'

To My Old Oak Table

75 *that vast gigantic dome* St Paul's Cathedral, London: compare Dickens's description at the end of chapter 19 ('Moving On') of *Bleak House*.

The Horkey

We have preserved the original italics, which Bloomfield uses to emphasise the energy of dialect speech. The notes which follow are by Bloomfield.

5   *Judie Twitchet* '[She] was a real person, who lived many years with my mother's cousin Bannock, at Honington'.

25   *hake* 'A sliding pot-hook'.

43   *cop't* 'Thrown'.

63   *sitch a mort* 'Such a number'.

89   *My Lord* 'The leader of the reapers'.

123 *gran'd* 'Strangled'.

133 *spirket* 'An iron hook'.

157 *for the nonce* 'For the purpose'.

162 *shanny-pated* 'Giddy, thoughtless'.

165 *skriggl'd* 'To struggle quickly'.

167 *quack'ling* 'Choaking'.

THE BROKEN CRUTCH

57-78 Compare John Clare's anti-enclosure poems, especially 'The Lamentations of Round Oak Waters' and 'To a Fallen Elm'.

90   *'Burnt-Hall'* Near Fakenham, 'a moated eminence, formerly the site of a mansion supposed to have been destroyed by fire' (Brayley, *Views in Suffolk*, pp. 43-4).

268 *suck'd a charming portion with a reed* Used a hollow reed as a drinking straw to siphon off enough wedding-ale ('a charming portion') to become intoxicated.

SHOOTER'S HILL

Shooter's Hill is near Woolwich, south-east London, on the old London to Dover high road. It commands 'a most extensive and variegated prospect, overlooking as large a city and as fine a country as any in the universe' (Brayley, *Views in Suffolk*, p. 53).

26   *Erith's ivied spire* The parish church of Erith, Kent, between Woolwich and Dartford on the south bank of the Thames, formerly a place of maritime importance, later a resort for Londoners.

60   *Surry-Hills* The North Downs.

64   *romantic Mole* The river Mole, flowing northwest through Sussex and Surrey to meet the Thames at East Molesey, opposite Hampton Court.

65   *Aye, there's the scene!* 'Box-Hill, and the beautiful neighbourhood of Dorking, in Surry' (RB).

89   *monumental tower* The triangular Tower at the summit of Shooter's Hill, commemorating the achievements of Sir William James (1721-83), who conquered the castle of Severndroog on the coast of Malabar, the stronghold of the pirate Angria, on 2 April 1755, part of 'a train of exploits of the highest moment to our mercantile transactions with the eastern world' (Brayley, *Views in Suffolk*, p. 53).

91   *Angria's subjugated power* See previous note. The first edition and the manuscript (British Library, Add. MS 28266, f. 29v) both have 'Angra'.

BARNHAM WATER

32   *The mighty 'City in the East.'* Thetford, Norfolk, an ancient town on the Icknield Way, capital of Saxon East Anglia, occupied by the Danes in 865, burnt by Sweyn in 1004, a bishopric from 1070 to 1094. It boasted at one time eight monasteries, including a famous Cluniac priory founded by Roger Bigod (d. 1107) in 1104. See Brayley, *Views in Suffolk*, pp. 31-3.

41   *Danish mounds* Earthworks raised by the invading Danes in 865.

55-6 *Bigods...Mowbrays...Framlingham* Framlingham Castle, Suffolk, now a ruin, was given to Roger Bigod (see note to l. 32), and became the principal stronghold of his descendants the Bigods, Mowbrays and Howards, earls and dukes of Norfolk.

The Banks of Wye

PREFACE TO THE BANKS OF WYE Text: first edition, 1811.
   a party of my good friends In a letter to his wife dated 16 August 1807 (Hart, no. 43), Bloomfield names the party as 'Mr. and Mrs. [Thomas Lloyd] Baker and self, Mr. [Robert Bransby] Cooper, and two daughters and two sons, with Miss Ewen, the governess'.

ADVERTISEMENT TO THE SECOND EDITION Text: corrected second edition, 1813.

JOURNAL OF A TOUR DOWN THE WYE Text: *Remains* (1824), II, pp. 25-8.
   sociables Open, four-wheeled carriages with six seats.

THE BANKS OF WYE Text: corrected second edition, 1813.

21   *Pen-y-vale* 'The respective heights of these mountains above the mouth of the Gavany, was taken barometrically by Gen. Roy.   Feet.
   The summit of the Sugar-Loaf 1852
   Of the Blorenge...1720
   Of the Skyrid ....1492' (RB).

44   *holy fame* 'There still remains, on the summit of the Skyrid, or St. Michael's Mount, the foundation of an ancient chapel, to which the inhabitants formerly ascended on Michaelmas Eve, in a kind of pilgrimage. A prodigious cleft, or separation in the hill, tradition says, was caused by the earthquake at the crucifixion, it was therefore termed the Holy Mountain' (RB).

'Song' ['The Man in the Moon'] Text: *Remains*, I, pp. 59-60.

Tune.—Ligoran Cosh An Irish jig. Francis O'Neill in *Waifs and strays of Gaelic melody* (second enlarged edition, Chicago: Lyon and Healy, *c.* 1922), traces this tune to 'Aird's Selections 1782-97'. Its correct Gaelic title is 'Ligrum Cus' ('Let go my foot'). According to O'Neill (a Chicago police captain who traced Irish tunes from recent immigrants in the 1920s) the title 'may also relate to the rent question'. (For this information we are indebted to Barry Bloomfield, and to the Irish Traditional Folk Archive, 63 Merion Square, Dublin 2). O'Neill gives the tune as follows (no.120):

'Sonnet. To Fifteen Gnats' Text: *Remains*, I, p. 31.

'Hob's Epitaph' Text: *Remains*, I, pp. 33-4. 'Hob' is a familiar form of Robert or Robin, often used to indicate either a rustic bumpkin, or a hobgoblin, puck or Robin Goodfellow. This 'Hob' seems to be a wizard's 'familiar'.

4   *exciseman* An officer employed to collect excise duty and prevent evasion of duty. Bloomfield no doubt intends a topical satirical reference to one or more of the (highly unpopular) measures to raise the excise on alcoholic drinks in the early nineteenth century. Cf. 'The Invitation,' ll. 127-30 and 210, in *May-Day with the Muses*.

9   *gauging* Ascertaining the content or capacity of a cask by measurement and calculation. In Bloomfield's time the main concern was with curbing the common practice of watering beers and spirits, tested by taking their specific gravity.

12   *supervisor* A Supervisor of the Excise, who would oversee and check the records of lower-ranking excise officers.

May-Day with the Muses Text: first edition, 1822.

PREFACE

T. Park Thomas Park (1759-1834), antiquary, bibliographer and poet, whom Bloomfield had known since at least 1801.

Cunningham's 'Kate of Aberdeen' Allan Cunningham (1784-1842), miscellaneous writer and friend to Hogg and Clare, wrote a number of popular 'old' Scottish ballads of this kind, some of which were included in R.H. Cromek's *Remains of Nithsdale and Galloway Song* (1810).

Dibdin's 'Sailor's Journal' Thomas John Dibdin (1771-1841), actor and dramatist, prolific writer and producer of popular plays, operas, poems and songs, many on patriotic themes.

THE INVITATION

38 *Oakly Hall* 'The seat of Sir Ambrose is situated in the author's imagination only; the reader must build Oakly Hall where he pleases' (RB).

209 *its costly store* Port wine, a luxury item imported from Portugal.

210 *well tax'd* See the note to 'Hob's Epitaph', l. 4, above.

211 *Lusitanian mountains* The mountains of Portugal (after the name of the Roman province of Lusitania which included the area of modern Portugal).

212 *Gama* The explorer Vasco Da Gama (*c.* 1469-1525) set off from Lisbon on his famous journey eastward on 8 July 1497.

227 *domestics* indigenous plants.

THE DRUNKEN FATHER

496 *Wilkie* David Wilkie (1785-1841), painter: see Introduction.

THE FORESTER

510 *Old Salcey Forest* An ancient royal forest covering 1,850 acres, a few miles south-east of Northampton.

579 *Clermont's bowers* Claremont Park, Esher, Surrey, where Princess Charlotte Augusta (1796-1817) died after giving birth to a still-born boy on 6 November 1817. See Stephen C. Behrendt, *Royal Mourning and Regency Culture: Elegies and Memorials of Princess Charlotte* (London: Macmillan, 1997).

622 *Bewick's* Thomas Bewick (1753-1828), wood-engraver. His illustrations of animals and birds include the engravings for the *General History of Quadrupeds* (1790), and the *History of British Birds* (1797 and 1804).

Hazelwood Hall (1823) Text: first edition, 1823.

'Glee for three voices' from Act II, Scene iii, p. 34.

'Simple Pleasures' from Act III, Scene iii, pp. 58-9. This title is from later editions of Bloomfield: in the text of Hazelwood Hall it is simply 'Air (Morrison).'

The Bird and Insect's Post-Office (1824) Text: *Remains,* II, pp. 138-41. 'The Author's Epitaph' does not appear in the printed text, and is taken from the title page of the manuscript (British Library, Add. MS. 30809, f. 11).

INDEX OF POETRY TITLES AND FIRST LINES